OUR FATHER'S JOURNEY

A PATH OUT OF POVERTY

Harry J. Deitz Jr.
As told by **Harry J. Deitz**

WITH CONTRIBUTIONS BY
Barbara C. Yates and Terry L. Deitz

LOCAL HISTORY
PRESS
an imprint of Sunbury Press, Inc.
Mechanicsburg, PA USA

LOCAL HISTORY
PRESS

an imprint of Sunbury Press, Inc.
Mechanicsburg, PA USA

For information about special discounts for bulk purchases, please contact Sunbury Press Orders Dept. at (855) 338-8359 or orders@sunburypress.com.

To request one of our authors for speaking engagements or book signings, please contact Sunbury Press Publicity Dept. at publicity@sunburypress.com.

FIRST LOCAL HISTORY PRESS EDITION: December 2021

Set in Adobe Garamond Pro | Interior design by Crystal Devine | Cover by Lawrence Knorr | Edited by Lawrence Knorr.

Publisher's Cataloging-in-Publication Data
Names: Deitz Jr., Harry J., author | Deitz, Harry J., author.
Title: Our father's journey : a path out of povery / Harry J. Deitz Jr. and Harry J. Deitz.
Description: First trade paperback edition. | Mechanicsburg, PA : Local History Press, 2021.
Summary: There was little hope for Harry Joseph Deitz when he was born into poverty in the Anthracite Coal Region at the start of the Great Depression. After his father was seriously hurt in a mine accident, his mother scrubbed floors to support a family of eight. But Harry was determined to change his fate to become successful and respected—and he did.
Identifiers: ISBN : 978-1-62006-878-6 (softcover).
Subjects: BIOGRAPHY & AUTOBIOGRAPHY / Editors, Journalists, Publishers | BIOGRAPHY & AUTOBIOGRAPHY / Cultural, Ethnic & Regional / General | FAMILY & RELATIONSHIPS / General.

Product of the United States of America
0 1 1 2 3 5 8 13 21 34 55

Continue the Enlightenment!

This memoir is dedicated to
Beverly J. (Smith) Deitz, wife, mother, and
grandmother, who loved us unconditionally
and made each of us a better person.

On the cover: You can tell how poor we were when you look at this photo and notice that a large hole in the right shoulder of the sweater was retouched by me or someone in the family. I don't remember when the photo was taken, but from the overall appearance, I would guess it was taken when I was either in second, third, or fourth grade. I assume it was one of the times when professional photographers came to the elementary schools and took individual photos of the students and teacher and sometimes group photos of classes. —Harry Sr.

Contents

Foreword

God sometimes works in mysterious ways. When he takes one life, he gives you another. In some cases, it is losing a cherished family member, who is replaced with a new baby at a later date. In a way, this story is about the loss of our wonderful mother, who gave us the rebirth of our dad.

Mom died in May 2020. In her final days, she told my brother Harry and me: "You'll have to take care of your dad. He'll be lost without me." That was a tough request she left us with because we never had as close of a relationship with dad as we had with mom. Dad was the family breadwinner, and his work life seemed to be his very existence.

After mom passed, nightly Facetime sessions became a ritual that we all came to cherish. Little by little, we began to view our father in a different light. We saw a side of him we never knew while growing up. When my brother Harry decided to write Dad's story, we had no idea what an interesting and amazing life this man had lived.

Our mom had given us a blessing from beyond the grave. We began to understand why he worked so hard, endured unbelievable family hardships, and how he struggled to build a life that he would be proud of. Our family came to understand how those things defined the man we never knew and the priority he put on his work life versus his family life. In losing our beloved mother, we came to know our wonderful father and build a relationship that we thought would never exist.

Our Father's Journey is an account in dad's own words that has helped our family treasure the self-made man that he is. A man who, against all odds, loved his family so much that he sacrificed himself to give us a better life. I hope this story inspires you to rekindle a close family relationship with a loved one and understand that every story has two sides.

Our thanks to our mother, Beverly Deitz, who gave us this precious gift.

—Barbara (Deitz) Yates

Preface

Every life is a story that deserves to be written. Few, however, make it to the pages of a book. This one might not have, either. But, at the age of 92, my father agreed to share the story of his life, which began in poverty at the start of the Great Depression.

Despite many obstacles, he went on to have a very successful career as a newspaper photographer, reporter, and editor. He became a respected and well-known member of his community. He loved and was married to one woman for 70 years. And he had a major influence on the lives of his three children, Barbara Yates, Terry Deitz, and me.

Nothing was easy for our father, but that never stopped him. That determination is part of what he passed on to us.

We thank him for that. And we love him for what he became and who he is.

We had asked him to write his own story for several years, but he said he struggled to find the right words to put on paper, unlike what he had always done during his newspaper days. Then, one afternoon, late in 2020, he and I were sitting together in his living room, and he started to tell stories to me about when he was growing up. It was the best conversation I had ever had with him. I saw and heard a side of him that he had rarely shared. His words flowed.

Several weeks later, I told him I would send some questions to him and asked him if he would write his answers as if he were talking to me like he did that day. I said that might be a way for us to write his story together.

Through his answers, I've come to know my father in a new way and with a new appreciation. It's a story I'm honored to help find its way onto these pages.

Our father was born, raised, and lived most of his life in or near the Anthracite coal region community of Shamokin in northeastern Pennsylvania.[1] He grew up poor, the youngest son of a miner, and although he never worked in the mines, he never could escape that coal town. Nor did he want to.

During his nine decades on Earth, he went from having few opportunities and little hope to eventually enjoying a comfortable lifestyle.

As his firstborn child, my early life was difficult at times. Our family had a loving home life with the necessities, but there were few extravagances early on. Likely because of my father's childhood difficulties, he and I often clashed over priorities, responsibilities, and personal objectives, although I never had doubts that I was loved. But my challenges and frustrations were not close to what he experienced. It would be many years before I came to understand and fully appreciate him and the reasons for some of the things he did.

In compiling this book, I have come to realize the influence he has had on my life, from teaching me the importance of hard work and responsibility, to follow him into the newspaper business, and even to determine that I wanted to spend more time and have a closer relationship with my family than he had with his.

This is the story of his journey through life as he remembers it and mostly in his own words in responses to my questions, similar to how a newspaper reporter conducts an interview.

It is prefaced and summarized by the following column I wrote about him for Father's Day in 2012.

—Harry Jr.

Special Tribute to a Father Who Escaped Poverty (2012 column)[2]

Every time I hear or read about the issues of poverty in my community, I think of my father and his family.

He is proof that it's not only possible to live through poverty but also to escape it.

Dad's father was a coal miner. That's something I write with pride. Who among us works as hard or in as dangerous conditions as miners do? Every day meant putting his life at high risk. That risk caught up to him through a back injury.

After that, he spent some years as a watchman until cancer cut short his working years and eventually his life. I never really knew him because he died when I was two.

What I learned about him and the rest of my father's family growing up was that life was hard. Very hard.

Along the way came poverty. There were many days when molasses bread was their meal. My father wore hand-me-down clothes. There were no frills. No memorable family vacations.

As many people in poverty do, my father quit school and went to work. But for some reason, he went back to school. Then several years later, he quit again and joined the Army. He finally had a few dollars in his pocket, but he sent money home to his sister to help support his parents every month.

That time in the service turned out to be something good because it was in the Army where he learned to take photographs and developed an interest in newspaper work. Like so many in the military, my father learned a skill that would provide him with a way to make a living—and a way to escape poverty.

He did something else very important. When he returned from the service, he visited his high school principal. The following week he was back in high school. He became the first high school graduate in his family.

My father eventually gained a comfortable lifestyle, but he has never had it easy. He always has worked long and hard hours. When I was younger, I resented the time that he devoted to work rather than to his family. Years later, I came to believe it likely was out of fear that he could slip back into the life of poverty he had escaped. And, yet, I can't recall him saying, "Poor me."

In my younger years, we always had food on our table and other necessities, but we usually lacked the extras that many others around us enjoyed.

His expectations for his children always were high—not just to succeed, but never to waste or fail. I still recall one time, as a teenager, I had saved a few dollars and bought a record album. The reason for his anger at my decision was something I didn't understand until years later.

Even so, that mentality and approach to life became ingrained in me. I learned to be frugal, which my children unknowingly perceived as being cheap. In reality, it was a matter of always being careful, having a safety net, and never wasting or taking things for granted.

Nobody ever handed anything to my father. He worked hard for everything and expected me to do the same. He seldom just handed anything to me, but he provided so many opportunities. Which is what helped to make me the way I am today.

Is that bad? Not at all.

You see, my father would never have considered buying a cellphone when he couldn't put food on the table. Neither would I.

He never wasted money on fancy cars that cost more than he could afford. Neither have I.

He always made sure he never went too deeply into debt and had a little bit of savings for emergencies so he would never fall back into his childhood lifestyle. I've learned those things, too.

My father and I didn't always see eye to eye. We often clashed. That was in part why when I registered to vote, I picked the opposite party.

Through the years, he has mellowed. So have I. We understand each other so much better and agree more now than when we both were younger. So much so that on the day I turned 60, I changed my registration.

I am not my father. Not because I don't want to be, but because I never could be. I have come to not only appreciate who he is and what he has accomplished but to love him for those things, too.

The poverty my father knew and the struggles I experienced helped to shape us and our approach to life. They helped us to appreciate what we have. They are experiences I would have preferred to avoid, but they definitely had value.

As a result, we both are so much richer than we would have been if we had not experienced all those challenges in life.

1

Born into the Great Depression

The year was 1928, and the United States was unknowingly on the verge of its most challenging time since the Civil War. In the decade after the end of World War I, the Roaring Twenties had brought hope and sudden prosperity for some, despite the concerns of others over changing social and moral standards.

In that year, Herbert Hoover was elected as the 31st president and predicted: "We in America today are nearer to the final triumph over poverty than ever before in the history of any land."[3] Mickey Mouse appeared in Walt Disney's *Steamboat Willie* cartoon. Amelia Earhart became the first woman to fly across the Atlantic Ocean. Alexander Fleming discovered penicillin.

And on April 30, in a small rented house in Coal Township, Pennsylvania, which surrounds what was then the borough of Shamokin, life began for Harry Joseph Deitz. It was one of the final joys for a family that, like many others, would soon know the true meanings of hardship and poverty.

Life was about to become difficult for those who were comfortable— and almost impossible for those who already were struggling like the Deitz family.

The youngest of six children, our father grew up during the ensuing Great Depression in a community that had expanded and eventually declined with the Anthracite coal industry. It was a hard life for many, including our father's family, even without the Depression. Mine owners amassed vast riches while their workers often struggled to pay rent and feed their families.

And yet, it was a safe and beautiful community, despite the coal dirt that covered streets and washed into the backyards of houses that sat at the base of the giant culm bank that bordered the north side of Shamokin and still casts a shadow over the community. Families and neighborhoods were tightly knit, even those that struggled with poverty. They shared time and supported each other at the many churches where they learned to live with their circumstances and at the many bars where they tried to forget their problems. It was only a slight exaggeration when people said there was a church and a bar on every block.

Shamokin, like other Anthracite coal region communities, grew into a small city with a mixture of immigrants from European countries such as Germany, England, Italy, Ireland, Poland, Lithuania, and Wales, who sought opportunities in a new land and were willing to work hard in the mines and textile mills and on farms to provide for their families.

They took pride in their community, where Thomas Alva Edison ran the Edison Illuminating Company of Shamokin, and St. Edward's became the first church to have electricity. Where Stan Coveleski escaped the mines by learning to pitch a baseball by throwing rocks at tin cans, which led to a Hall of Fame baseball career. Where the Eagle Silk Mill became the largest textile building under one roof in the United States. And where the large mountain of culm was somewhat proudly referred to as the largest manmade mountain in the world.

For many, being a Coal Cracker was both an honor and a curse. That was the setting into which our father was born. Despite the difficulties, it was a special place for our father. It was home.

Three of his four grandparents were immigrants from Germany and Austria and had little formal education. Our father became the first in his family to graduate from high school. Even that wasn't easy because of the need to help support his family. Twice he quit school, but both times he returned.

His father, Harry, was born in Washington, D.C., in 1883. He eventually would find his way to Shamokin, where he worked at the local Cameron Colliery until he was seriously injured in a mining accident in 1930 that left him unable to do physical work. And yet, he lived another 24 years until the age of 71.

His mother, Christine, was born in 1896 on the family farm in Shamrock Mills, a short distance from Shamokin. She was a strong and hard-working woman who did housework at home and for others and cleaning for several companies to provide a meager existence for her family. She lived for 102 years.

Together, they raised six children—Dave, Clyde, Quilla, Ben, Lew, and Harry—although their family life lacked the closeness and warmth our father would come to know after he married Beverly Smith in 1949. Because mining work did not provide the resources they needed to support a family of eight, they moved in with Joe Bray, a widowed friend who lived alone in a large old house in Tharptown.

And yet, despite their unfortunate circumstances and the limited supervision and direction they provided, Harry and Christine Deitz instilled—perhaps unknowingly—something in our father that would not only help to lift him out of poverty but also would set him on a path where he would gain respect in his profession and community, come to understand the closeness in a family and develop a deep faith in God.

HARRY JR.: Tell me about the house where you were born.

HARRY SR.: It was a small two-and-a-half-story home on South Oak Street in Coal Township. It had a kitchen and living room on the first floor and three small rooms on the second with no bath. Space on the top floor that was an attic was used as a bedroom for two of the boys. I understand I was delivered by our family doctor at the time named Dr. Benjamin Bealor, who had an office on Sixth Street. He was a typical country doctor whose business was mostly making house calls.

HARRY JR.: You were named after your father, who didn't have a middle name. Why did your parents wait to give that name to their youngest? Why is your middle name Joseph?

HARRY SR.: I have no clue. Several years ago, I needed a copy of my birth certificate and contacted the Bureau of Vital Statistics. The records showed my middle name as Albert. A correction was requested and approved because I had been using Joseph for as long as I could remember.

HARRY JR.: *A possible connection to the name Joseph could be from his mother's grandfathers—Joseph Sumberich (or Sumberacz) and Joseph Pesanka. The name Sumberich became Sunbury when her father, Anthony, emigrated from Austria late in the 19th Century. There is no known connection to the name Albert.*

How poor were you growing up? Did the family receive public assistance?

HARRY SR.: There was no question about it. As a family of eight, with dad earning a minimal wage as a miner, things were tough making ends meet. There was rent to pay and food to buy, but very little income. I think we got some help from sympathetic neighbors, but that too was very limited and periodic.

Sometime previously, mom had befriended a widower from Tharptown named Joseph Bray. When he heard of our family's plight, he offered mom and dad a deal to move in with him in a 12-room house he owned. It was the answer to part of our financial problems to exist as a family. There was an arrangement that mom and dad would eventually become owners of the property.

Some adjustments had to be made by the older children attending public grade schools in the western section of Coal Township, except David, who was, I believe, a sophomore in Coal Township's new high school on Juniper Street. After we moved to Tharptown sometime around 1929, I know Quilla, and I believe Ben, attended what was then the antiquated Tharptown Elementary School, about a block away from where we now lived.

A short time after we moved, mom and dad applied for public assistance, but I believe it was not enough to take care of what we needed. We had a place to live, but we didn't have many common necessities other families had, including scheduled meals, new clothing, and new shoes.

Even affording coal as fuel to heat part of that three-story home was a problem. I remember family members going up the nearby mountain to pick coal on culm banks and discarded piles of unsalable coal at some abandoned mining operations, placing it in buckets and burlap bags and carrying it down into the valley of Tharptown where our new way of life was unfolding. The life we originally knew took a turn downward toward a life in poverty after dad's accident.

I watched Dolly Parton one night recently on television talking about her life. She grew up in the Ozarks. She had a big family. Her life was

The only known photograph of Harry Joseph Deitz as a toddler, probably taken in 1929.

like mine. Exactly. She had a big family, and her father was poor, and her mother was poor, and she had seven or eight brothers and sisters. A good comparison between us.

I remember mostly the hard times—no special holidays, no birthday celebrations, very few nutritious meals, desiring and even coveting the things that other kids my age had.

HARRY JR.: Tell me about your father. He was born in Washington, D.C. Why was his family living there? Why did they move to Llewellyn, where he grew up? What was his personality? Did you spend much time together? How did he meet your mother?

HARRY SR.: His father, my grandfather, was some kind of a firefighter in Washington. Dad's family apparently moved to the Llewellyn area in Schuylkill County when he was very young. I don't know how he ended up at Llewellyn. He was confirmed in a church there, and they spelled his name Deats. That's where my grandmother came from, Sarah Starr.

HARRY JR.: *Dad's grandfather, Karl Maximillian Dietz, born around 1845 in Germany, died around 1887, about four years after his son, Harry, was born. Max's wife, the former Sarah Ann Starr, moved back to Llewellyn, Schuylkill County, where she had been born in 1840. Harry still was living with her in Llewellyn when the 1910 census was taken.*

HARRY SR.: But we can't fill in the gap between that time and his obtaining employment as a miner at what was then called the Cameron Colliery outside of Shamokin. We know he stayed at an inn located along Route 122 (now Route 61) in the heart of Paxinos. That's where he met mom, who worked there as a maid or a domestic.

Dad (at 30) was a lot older than 18-year-old Christine Sunbury, but they apparently had a relationship that culminated in their marriage by Squire Harrison Heslop (justice of the peace) of Shamokin on February 14, 1914.

Dave was born later that summer. Dad and mom initially resided in a half double on First Street in Shamokin, then moved to the small house on Oak Street where the other five children were born.

In March 1930, he was injured in a mining accident at the Glen Burn (Cameron Colliery at that time) and had to give up any kind of manual work. I was born in 1928 when we still lived in the house on Oak Street, and dad was hurt in March of 1930, only a short time after we had moved in with Joe at Tharptown.

I knew him as being a very quiet person who was uneducated but, at first, a dedicated provider for his family. He kept to himself quite a bit yet would help anyone who needed help. I think he tried his very best to be a good husband and provider but was limited by complications from the back injuries he suffered.

Although he was not at home much, spending the bulk of his time at the Union Fire Company, he commanded obedience and respect and used his belt to get it in some cases.

MINER BADLY HURT IN FALL DOWN MANWAY

Harry Deitz of Tharptown, in Hospital in Serious Condition Result of Thrilling Plunge in Cameron Workings

Harry Deitz, well known resident of Tharptown, was seriously injured at 11:30 this morning when he was hurled down a manway and buried under a succeeding rush of coal and rock. He is in the Shamokin State Hospital, the victim of severe contusions of the head, chest, back and abdomen and internal injuries.

Deitz was employed as a miner in a heavy pitching breast and when coal blocked the manway proceeded to effect its release. A heavy lump of coal tumbled down the manway, striking Deitz and releasing quantities of coal and rock. As he fell into the pocket he was partly covered by the rush, thus suffering extensive injuries.

Speedy rescue of the man was effected by other workmen, he was then given first aid treatment at the emergency hospital and then rushed to the hospital where surgeons consider his conditions as quite serious.

The victim is one of Tharptown's best known residents and is a miner of vast experience.

Condition Of Mine Victim Is Favorable

Harry Deitz, of Tharptown, who was severely injured when knocked down a manway at the Cameron colliery shortly before noon yesterday, was said by the surgeons at the Shamokin state hospital to be resting quite comfortably today.

It was widely rumored last evening that Dietz had suffered a broken back but this is denied by the hospital staff, although the young man received severe injuries across the back. He is bruised and lacerated from head to knees and is also suffering internal injuries, although no bones were broken in the mishap.

Dietz has many friends who will be pleased to know that his injuries are not as serious as rumor would have had them immediately following the accident.

Shamokin News-Dispatch stories about mine accident, from March 28 (Page 1, above left) and March 30, 1930.

Rare photo of Harry Dietz, our dad's father, in 1953, a year before he died.

Dad was not a real family man, although he tried to provide.

He lived because he was a fireman, the social end of it. He spent many, many hours at the firehall. He'd go over there as soon as he got up sometimes, and he'd be there all day. I think he had some kind of agreement with them that he did some domestic or maintenance work, and they gave him his meals. He was always at the hosey, and they called it the hosey. He was there day and night. In fact, I can't remember him sitting down and having a meal with us. We never sat down to a meal that I recall. It was something we all picked up on the run. It was a strange family.

He chewed tobacco all the time, and I think that was his downfall. I think that's how he got cancer of the colon. He always had a chew in his mouth. And that was because chewing tobacco was a way that miners helped to fight off dust, coal dust, in the mines. It was a way of life.

HARRY JR.: Did he go to school?

HARRY SR.: I think he went to school in the Llewellyn area while his parents or maybe just his mother lived in Schuylkill County.

HARRY JR.: *The 1940 census listed my grandfather having a first-grade education and my grandmother as second grade.*

During World War II, my dad's father had to register with the draft board on April 27, 1942. He was 59 at the time. It listed his height at 5-6 1/2 and his weight at 140 pounds, with brown eyes, brown hair, and a light complexion.

"He was small featured, had no teeth, but chewed tobacco all the time," my father recalled.

Interestingly, his name on the registration card was spelled Harry Deitz, but his signature was Harry Dietz.

"I think the spelling of Deitz was actually right," dad told me. "Somewhere along the line, it got reversed, probably when mom, who had very little if any education, signed important papers some time or other."

At some point, the family name was changed to Deitz from Dietz, but no one in the family knows when, why, or how. It continues to cause confusion on documents to this day.

Do you remember anything about your father getting hurt in the mine?

HARRY SR.: I was too young to remember anything about that. I was only two years old. The account I read in a logbook at the Knoebels (mining) museum carried information about it. I think he had a severe back injury and was hospitalized at what was then known as the State Hospital for Miners at Shamokin. He recuperated at home for a long while after his discharge from the hospital.

HARRY JR.: He lived 24 years after the accident. Did he do any other work after that, other than at the Fire Company?

HARRY SR.: I don't think he did any physical work. He sold tickets at one of the rides when a carnival came to Tharptown as a fund-raising event sponsored by the fire company. As a physical therapy, he sawed wood almost every morning and evening between visits to the hosey, where he spent long hours sometimes into the evening.

HARRY JR.: Do you have any memories of doing things with him or spending time together?

HARRY SR.: There were few if any times that we spent together. One of those rare times I remember was when he wanted to do something special for me after he had earned some money, either selling scrap or doing some extra work at the hosey. He took me to town for a pair of clodhopper shoes. That's the only time I remember we did anything together while I was young and still at home.

HARRY JR.: What did he do if he was at home in the evening?

HARRY SR.: Like the rest of the family, he listened to programs on the radio, among which was the 7 p.m. newscast by I think the name was Lowell Thomas. Other programs that he liked were *The Shadow, Mr. Keen, Tracer of Lost Persons*, (The Adventures of) *Ellery Queen*, and *The Green Hornet*.

HARRY JR.: Did he ever drive or own a car?

HARRY SR.: He never had that luxury, nor did he ever have a driver's license or bank account. I think he got workman's comp for a year after the accident, then no compensation of any kind.

HARRY JR.: Tell me about your mother. Was she warm and nurturing? Where was she born? Where did she grow up? What kind of relationship did you have?

HARRY SR.: Until she was married, mom lived on the farm in Paxinos (Shamrock Mills) and walked to school every day several miles. I don't think she had much of an education. She helped by doing chores on the farm and then worked at the inn when a young teenager.

She was born in the farmhouse built by her father, Anthony Sunbury, an immigrant (from Austria) who later became an American citizen. When her mother arrived here, she sold produce at the market in Shamokin. I assume mom helped with that.

Christine Deitz in 1953.

She was very motherly to me. I was her pride and joy.

I think mom was very warm and friendly, but she had a temper, too, if things didn't go her way. One of her problems was that if someone crossed her, she didn't forget. She was always concerned about my welfare and often took my side during any problem between me and dad or when I got into trouble.

I can't recall any time that she raised her voice to scold me for something I did. Instead, she would give me the silent treatment.

She worked for the Shamokin Packing Company. And she was a maintenance person at the Kempton Dress Shop. She scrubbed the floors and cleaned up. She was like a janitor. They put her on Social Security at the packing company, and it was enough that she got all the quarters she needed (for benefits). She got the minimum. Her Social Security was only about $400 or $500 a month. She cleaned the offices for the packing company.

HARRY JR.: Tell me about Joe Bray, who married your mother after your father died. What was your parents' relationship with him? What was your relationship with him?

HARRY SR.: From what I learned years ago, Joe and his family were lifetime or near-lifetime residents of Tharptown, owning real estate that included the 12-room, two-and-one-half story, wood-frame dwelling on the back unpaved street overlooking the center of the town. He was very prominent, one of the organizers of Union Fire Company, a Coal Township fire chief, and an active fire warden for the Pennsylvania Department of Conservation Forestry Division.

I don't know when he met mom and dad, but I think it might have been shortly after the death of his wife, Mary, in 1924. The story I heard was that Joe and several other men often visited Anthony Sunbury's farm during hunting season at the same time Mom was there, and she would invite the group in for coffee or refreshments.

When he heard of the family's hardships, he offered them a plan to move in with him and eventually own the property. In the meantime, he would provide some financial help. I don't know the fine points of the agreement, but I do know there was something about a mortgage with a building and loan company at a very minimal monthly payment ($12), to which everyone in the family contributed one way or another.

He worked for a guy named Alvin Venn, who built a big coal breaker on a vacant lot. Al Venn used to pay me a quarter to help pick slate at the breaker. One time they asked me to push the coal down from up above on the hopper, and I did. And, boy, if they wouldn't have grabbed me, I would have gone into that crusher that crushed the coal. They were at

Christine and Joe Bray, circa 1960.

the bottom, right at the opening, and both of them grabbed my arms and kept me from going into the roller. The coal went on a conveyer up to a shaker, and it was sorted on this screen.

Joe also was a laborer for Mertz Motors. Dad worked there later when they established a used car lot. Dad worked there for about the last three or four years of his life. He was a night watchman, but he spent most of his time at the hosey.

Joe was like a family member, treating all the kids like they were his own. I think Joe and mom were real close, even when dad lived. I think dad accepted it as something that happened. I hate to put my mom down. She did keep the family together. And Joe helped. He bought the first radio we had. Any place mom went, Joe took her because he had a car. It was the only way she could survive, and she did her best.

HARRY JR.: *In addition to Joe, some boarders lived with the family at times to help pay the bills. Dad's father died from colon cancer on May 8, 1954, at age 71. His mother and Joe married on May 14, 1955. Joe was the same age as dad's father, 12 years older than Christine.*

Tell me about the house where you grew up in Tharptown.

HARRY SR.: It sat on a hill with the back entrance overlooking the center of Tharptown. Actually, it was a double home, converted to a single with two entrances facing a hill in what appeared to be the back end of the house but was actually the front. There were two entrances on that level with an unpaved road that curved down a hill on the left side to a street at the bottom of the property. There was one entrance at the top of the yard leading to a basement kitchen on the right side and another room on the left side, with steps between them leading to the second floor. Altogether, there were 12 rooms, two on ground level at the rear, facing Tharptown, four on each of the second and third floors, and a two-room attic.

There was running water in the basement kitchen. We didn't have a bathroom. No toilet facilities. We had an outhouse. It was cold in the wintertime.

Around the western side and back of the house, a large porch provided access to two doors on the second floor. During the fall and winter months, heat was provided by a coal stove in the basement kitchen and a space heater in one room on the second floor.

There was a concrete sidewalk extending from the kitchen entrance on the ground floor the entire length of a yard. On the right side of the sidewalk was an outhouse. In front of that was a steel-fence enclosure in which chickens were raised. On the left side of the walk was an open area the entire length of the yard, which was used for raising vegetables in the spring and summer.

At the bottom of the yard, off one of the main streets, was a little wooden structure that had a kitchen on one floor and a large bedroom on the second floor. It served as living quarters for a three-member family.

HARRY JR.: *Dad knew the part of Coal Township where he grew up as Tharptown, but the area also is referred to as Uniontown and Gosstown.*

After Joe died in 1963, dad's mother lived alone in the old house until around 1966, when it was razed as part of the highway project to expand Route 61 to four lanes and bypass the center of Tharptown. She moved into a trailer at the bottom of her yard, where she had an indoor bathroom for the first time in her life, and she lived there until she went into the county-run nursing home in 1993. She died at 102 in 1999, a year short of living in three centuries.

What were your family meals like growing up? Did you eat together? Did you have enough food? What do you remember your mother making?

HARRY SR.: A full-course dinner, most times on a Sunday, was a luxury meal made possible only after mom had saved enough from working during weekdays, getting 50 cents or a dollar as a cleaning woman or washing clothing for some residents in the Tharptown area.

The occasional meal consisted of meat, fried or mashed potatoes or baked beans, and a vegetable, most likely red beets or green lettuce. Mostly it was what mom could get together, either leftovers or whatever food was on hand, but that was never much. Most times, the ingredients for a meal came from mom and Joe going to the butcher shops or corner grocery stores and seeing what items were on sale before buying. I know it often was the cheapest meat, but mom made the meal like an experienced cook would because she learned from her dad's family when they lived on the farm in the Shamrock area of Shamokin Township. As an example of substituting, she liked to make pork and sauerkraut, but the price of a pork roast was more than she could afford, so she made a substitution. Instead of a pork roast, it was made with pigtails, which were considerably cheaper but served a purpose just as well.

Growing up, I remember we seldom ate together as a family but grabbed on the run anything available. One of my favorites many times during the week was a peanut butter and molasses or jelly sandwich. One of the delicacies was a mushroom sandwich made with wild mushrooms picked in the forest near our new home. The same forest was a mecca for wild berries that we would pick, take home, wash and clean, and give to mom. If we were lucky, we'd have a piece of a tasty pie as something special. We were fortunate to have a special fruit too. There were two rows of grape vines extending from the basement kitchen door to halfway down the backyard.

HARRY JR.: What were holidays like, especially Christmas? What about birthdays?

HARRY SR.: I can truthfully say I knew Christmas was all about the birth of Jesus Christ because as a pupil in the first grade, I would join others in singing carols at the appropriate time of the year. I remember being selected for a role in one of the Christmas plays because I had a fairly good singing voice for a youngster. My small part was representing the king on the way to present a gift of myrrh to the Christ child and singing a verse of the carol, "We Three Kings." Being selected for a part in the Christmas play or any other event like singing "Here Comes Santa Claus" was a big honor because it was one of the ways of celebrating the holiday without the traditional exchange of gifts, something we couldn't afford.

Christmas in our house was a little different than that observed at almost every other home along the main street and back alleys, where each year strings of blinking lights adorned porches and front doors. It was no one's fault that my sister, four brothers, and I didn't get traditional toys or new clothing for Christmas. Simply, the family didn't have the money. But mom made up for it by cooking a delicious turkey or chicken dinner, usually selecting one of the roosters from the large enclosed pen in our yard.

But it was fun to participate in an event such as the annual Christmas play, complete with singing and costumes and portraying characters from the Biblical story of Christ's birth. Like the events at Christmas time, other school plays and programs were presented by students for the general public in an auditorium at the front of a converted area of the school's basement. A wooden stage and curtain on a wire stretched across one end. Folding chairs were used for seating.

Sometimes movies, shown using a 16mm projector, were offered at night as entertainment for residents of Tharptown. One I distinctly recall was the 1930s version of *Frankenstein*, starring Boris Karloff. It scared the life out of me, and later that night, I slept with my head under the covers. I recall that some other popular movies were shown at the cost of 10 cents in the auditorium on a specified afternoon or night each week by a private resident on approval by the school board.

The Christmas plays each year always drew large audiences, including parents of the student participants. There were other programs of educational interest as well as the performances of professional actors and athletes strictly as periodic assemblies for the elementary students.

But, while other families in the community shared the joy and spirit of Christmas, with the exchange of gifts and fun and laughter, the celebration in our home was much more subdued.

And birthdays weren't any different. In fact, the particular days earmarked as birthdays for family members came and went without fanfare or any other celebration. If any of the siblings were lucky enough to get an article of used clothing as a hand-me-down from a friend or neighbor, it was considered a gift for one's birthday. We didn't need special gifts, although we did get some from sympathetic friends and neighbors to remind us of God's gifts for survival.

HARRY JR.: Did you attend church and Sunday school as a child? Were you religious then?

HARRY SR.: I attended Sunday school periodically. But I don't think I went to church. The Sunday school teacher was Miss Killinger, and the superintendent was George Frederick. I remember that I was interested in learning the Bible and answered a question once about Jonah and received a plastic whale as a reward. It was a prized possession of mine for many years and occupied a special place on the buffet in one of the second-floor rooms of the house.

I also remember going to Knoebel's (Amusement Park) on a large passenger bus for a Sunday school picnic. Mom took me to the old schoolhouse west of the church on a corner lot where the two-story building stood and Sunday school was held. Two pretty, young high school girls were put in charge of me on the bus ride and for the picnic. The good food was a treat, and we were given tickets for the rides and attractions. But I found another interest—I played in the shallow creek in the back of the pavilion where our picnic was held. By the end of the day, I was tired and fell asleep on the bus back to Tharptown.

HARRY JR.: Did you have chores as a child at home?

HARRY SR.: Growing up was difficult in a family of eight without much of an income for food, clothing, and even entertainment. My mother tried very hard to be the leader in our home after dad's injuries, but by doing what work she did outside the family to earn very little compensation, most of which was used to buy food, there wasn't a lot of time at home to delegate responsibilities to the younger children, including myself.

But she was protective in every way and defended us when any problem arose, including some corporal punishment by our dad. I think mom kind of took command herself when something had to be done, rather than delegate to any of us.

She was a peach, a loving mother who cared for every one of us until we left home as young adults to be on our own. The upbringing of the children at home was a rough chore of her own, and she tried very hard at that until she got help in the 1930s when her mom, my grandmother, Rosie Sunbury, came to live with us about six or seven years after the death of mom's father, Rosie's husband, Anthony Sunbury, my grandfather.

HARRY JR.: As the youngest child, did your siblings interact with you early in your life?

HARRY SR.: I don't think any of my brothers and my sister interacted closely. Most were on their own in whatever they did or didn't do, including myself, whether their activity, motivations, or their ambitions were good or not so good. Except for David, who was the oldest and most reserved, and Benny, who in my opinion was the smartest and always the most eager to learn, as evidenced by his earning honor roll status during almost all of his high school marking periods, all of us were on our own in what was a poverty situation where you had to earn anything you wanted or needed by self-motivation.

HARRY JR.: Which of your siblings were you closest to?

HARRY SR.: If any, it was Ben during my early childhood, and later during my early teen years, Clyde took a little interest in me. But, basically, none of us were very closely associated in individual activity or anything else as what you see in other close-knit families in a small community.

HARRY JR.: With which of your siblings didn't you get along?

HARRY SR.: No question about that. For some reason or another, Lew actually was over-jealous of me to the point of continuously down-grading everything I did and exerting physical harm whenever he wanted the upper hand, especially during my early teens. We had many fights, not the brotherly encounters that all was forgotten afterward, but some that harbored hatred toward each other.

Christine and Harry Deitz with their grown children in the only known family photo, taken on May 25, 1953, about a year before Harry died. Standing left to right: Harry, Lew, Clyde, Quilla, Dave, and Ben. Our father was 25 at the time.

It was a strange relationship that I could never understand. It reached a point of hatred, leading to many incidents of violence with each of us not realizing that what we did during uncontrolled emotional outbursts could have resulted in serious permanent injury to both of us. He was several years older than me and held the upper hand as the most aggressive, and definitely had the better physical abilities to emerge the winner every time we engaged in any combative arguments.

Both of us were still in grammar school when the conflicts began to materialize. Why did it happen? I have no idea, but I think it was because he enjoyed popularity as a member of the band and as a successful little businessman selling bags of potato chips, pretzels, and candy house to house in the town. His popular image might have been threatened when I came on the scene and became a paperboy, passing the Harrisburg and (Williamsport) *Grit* papers to many of his same customers.

And he had another problem involving his eyesight. He was afflicted by what was called cross-eyes and, at an early age, had to wear glasses until he underwent surgery at Philadelphia's Wills Eye Hospital to correct the problem. That surgery and the trip were paid for by a couple he had befriended, who knew the financial situation involving our entire family.

Lew also was befriended by state highway patrol members whose quarters were in a home on Route 122, the main road through the town, across the street from the former schoolhouse. They would often give him some change and candy from slot machines they confiscated during raids on businesses where the machines were used illegally according to state laws at the time.

But, while people liked him, they were unaware that he was a bully, especially to his younger brother.

Lew's attitude toward me seemed to change after his surgery, but the punishment I took and my response with similar violence were unforgettable. I couldn't forget when he punched me in the face for no reason, and I had a black eye for five days. Or an incident when he got so mad at me that he wrapped a curtain-rod rope around my neck, or his grabbing me and throwing me in a swimming hole in a stream in the watershed across the creek east of the community. And each time, I responded by punching and kicking and throwing objects at him, including silverware that was within reach. Fortunately, he was never hurt by the flying objects.

It wasn't long after his surgery that things turned around. The violence ended with both of us treating each other as blood brothers. Eventually, I helped him after he obtained a job as a bread slicer and wrapper at a bakery on the main street of the community. I operated the slicing machine, and he operated the wrapper during the early morning hours when the bread loaves were delivered to grocery stores.

Lew and I remained brotherly friends for the rest of our lives until his death in 1982 from stomach cancer in Pompano Beach, Florida, where he successfully owned and operated an appliance sales and repair business for many years.

HARRY JR.: Tell me about your earliest memory.

HARRY SR.: I think it was soon after we moved in with Joe in Tharptown. I was very young, but I recall Joe and someone else—I believe it was (my brother) Dave or Ben—mixing cement in a metal washtub at the bottom of the long yard for part of a walk. During that time, the nation was experiencing depression, and jobs were either non-existent or hard to find. My brother Dave and a friend would go up on the mountain and pick coal to sell. I remember they had a very small business arrangement but decided to construct a hand-operated coal shaker on property adjoining an access road a short distance into the woods from the main house. The coal shaker didn't last long for some reason, so Dave and his buddy hopped a freight to look for a job somewhere in the Midwest.

HARRY JR.: Where did you attend elementary school, and what do you remember about it?

HARRY SR.: On the very sunny morning of Tuesday, September 4, 1934,[4] the mischievous Harry Deitz, age 6, walked hand-in-hand with his sister down the main street and reluctantly entered the yellow-brick Uniontown Grammar School three blocks from his home. His sister didn't go into the building with him but left him at the door on the western side of the entrance over which the word "boys" was carved in the cement mantle. He followed the crowd up the steps to the first floor and entered the room on the front section marked first grade. His first teacher was a beautiful young lady named Olive Miller. But later in the day, he was sent to another room where the teacher of that class was Miss Catherine Dugan.

I made a couple of friends and thought that being in a crowd of 20 other students was pretty neat. I thought the teacher was very neat,

The 1934 Uniontown School first-grade class of Miss Dugan (standing at right). Harry Deitz is fourth from the left in the front row and shown in the blowup, below right.

Harry Deitz in an early school picture.

too, because she took a lot of time teaching us how to spell our name, the ABCs, and other things first-graders are usually taught. There was no cafeteria in the school, but we got an hour off for lunch, and most usually went home and had something to eat and then came back for the afternoon class that was broken up with a recess around 2:30 p.m., depending on the weather.

The principal for the eight grades was Adam Hancock, and the word was that he was pretty tough and demanded discipline, or else we would be subject to capital punishment that included spanking with a fictitious electric paddle. Some of the other teachers that I remember were Mary Kerstetter and Mamie Crone, second grade; Hannah Shultz, third grade; Harold Yocum, fourth grade; Mr. Burrell, fifth grade; Ralph Cramer, sixth grade; Victor Carter, fifth or sixth grade; Mr. Johns, seventh grade; and Mr. Hancock, eighth grade.

The large two-story, yellow-brick building was somewhat new compared to some of the other school buildings in Coal Township and Shamokin Borough. But the Coal Township School Board, composed of members elected by public vote every two years, took a big financial step by building three new buildings about the same time around 1928, including a four-year high school and two elementary educational facilities.[5] All were two-story, and all had a yellow-brick exterior. The new high school, built at Oak and Juniper streets in the western section of Coal Township, included a gymnasium on the eastern end and an auditorium on the western end. The new building allowed the board to split the four-year classes by scheduling students in the western section of the township to attend the new building for four years, while students in the eastern section attended the first two years in the former high school building at Springfield, then transferred to the new building on Juniper Street for their junior and senior years.

The new elementary schools were located along the main street in Tharptown (called the Uniontown school), replacing a two-story, red-brick building as old as the community itself, and in Ferndale in the heart of a growing residential section in the west end. Both were constructed on property that provided space for outdoor recreation activities that included baseball fields. Along with the new high school building, the elementary centers were beautiful additions to the two sections of the township.

I kind of liked school, and this was indicated by a perfect attendance record up to the fourth grade when I took one day off early in June for my maternal grandmother's funeral.

One of the things about grammar school was that we had a recess every afternoon. Instead of joining the other kids in playing baseball and other games during that time, I would run three blocks to my home for a snack. I would get back to school in plenty of time for the remainder of the afternoon session. My usual trek home brought a chuckle from all the teachers.

I was young then and not aware that the clothes I wore were hand-me-downs, some that others in the same school had worn previously. I was lucky that my mother and, with the help of Joe, purchased me brand-new brown and white dress shoes for my graduation from the eighth grade. The other articles of clothing were donated. I learned not to be ashamed but to accept with gratitude any donation of clothing that fit me. In fact, I was proud of one article, a reversible raincoat.

HARRY JR.: *The Uniontown school was built in 1925 and demolished in 1982, 17 years after the merger of the Shamokin and Coal Township school districts.*

Who were your friends as a child? Did other kids look down on you, or were many of them poor, too?

HARRY SR.: I was not a loner. I did have several boyhood friends. There were times when I felt left out, but we had a gang who did things together for the most part.

I had several friends at different times, including a gang of about seven who gathered for a hangout at night on the porch of a family living on the main street that included four girls, two of which were teenagers. My closest friends in that group were Robert "Duke" Culton and Theron "Bags" Woodley.

Bags' dad was an ice and coalman, and often he would take a group of us kids on a fishing trip. Two other good friends who were a little younger than me were Leo "Junior" Fisher and Richard Moore. During the summer months, we always found something to do—mostly go

Harry Jr.: This is one of my favorite pictures of my father's boyhood—a Coal Region version of a Huck Finn and Tom Sawyer type picture with his gang of friends from around the early 1940s with him right in the middle with a cigarette. I can only imagine the trouble this group would have gotten into, which ironically brings to mind and probably explains the strict upbringing I experienced growing up under my father. The photo was taken on the baseball field behind the school in Tharptown and they are sitting on a roller used on the field, but he doesn't know who would have taken it. He remembers Robert "Duke" Culton, Theron "Bags" Woodley, Bob Foulds, Jack Ford and "Shine" Betz, but he doesn't recall the last names of Charley or Bill.

swimming on hot days in a dam constructed by the older boys and some men on a stream across from the Shamokin sulfur creek on the property of the Roaring Creek Water Company. It was there my brother Lewey often threw me in the water. I had to learn to swim rather quickly.

When I was growing up, the two forms of entertainment were listening to the radio and going to the early evening showing of a movie at one of the theaters in town. Sometimes we got together for Saturday matinees at the Majestic. By paying 10 cents admission, we got a Monday ticket that allowed us admission to the theater the following Monday to see whatever film was being shown. The admission cost for the Monday show was five cents.

The summer also was highlighted by a carnival or circus coming to town and setting up an operation in the large field behind the school or at a racetrack in Weigh Scales. Duke and I once rode from Tharptown to Weigh Scales on a three-wheel bike to watch the men set up tents for two performances later in the day.

Duke also came from a poor family. His dad worked in the same mine where my father was injured. Like in my family's case, neighbors and close friends and relatives often helped out either by providing food or giving some small financial donations. Both of us often took on special jobs helping homeowners weed gardens, collecting scrap to sell to dealers who made their rounds once or sometimes twice a week, or doing whatever odd jobs were available, all for a pay of 10 or 20 cents.

At one time, I had a paper route for two metropolitan newspapers— the *Harrisburg News* and the *Williamsport Grit*. Two or three summers, I was a batboy for the Union Fire Company baseball team, and later I worked as a pin boy at the Elks Club's alleys in Shamokin and the Bowl-Mor along Route 122 between Paxinos and Weigh Scales. I got 10 cents a game as a batboy and 50 cents for setting up pins at the bowling alleys.

I'd take anything that came along. I used to collect iron or any junk. I'd collect it and sell it to the sheeny[6] when the sheeny would come around. I got a nickel or a dime for it. They'd have a thing they'd measure with a scale, and they'd give you so much a pound for clothes or so much a pound for brass. Brass and copper were the big things. They used to have trap shooting over at the water company, and we used to go over and get the shotgun shells and burn off the paper from the bottom part that was all brass.

HARRY JR.: Many of your boyhood friends had nicknames. Yours was Hamy. How did you get it?

HARRY SR.: I don't know. I tried to find that out, and I could never find that out. My friends, all of them, at the school, it was always Hamy Deitz. Hamy Deitz. They'd say, "Hamy Deitz is in trouble again." Everybody had nicknames. Duke and Bags and Butsy Tyler. Shine Betz. There were a lot of different ones.

Harry Joseph Deitz (center) with friends Richard Moore (left) and Leo "Junior" Fisher, circa 1940.

HARRY JR.: What and where did you play as a child?

HARRY SR.: We played cowboys and Indians most of the time and went to the movies when I was able to earn small change for hauling ashes or pulling weeds.

At one time, there was an open field with a cover of grass adjacent to the highway where a Tasty Freeze stand is now located. We would get teams together for a touch and sometimes a tackle football game. In addition to the open area adjacent to the highway, there were fields behind the school and in the back of the Union Fire Company building. It didn't matter what kind of games we played—baseball, football, soccer, or even one called kick the can—we were happy.

Leo Fisher lived on the main street, the same block, and we were pretty close. So one day, we got the idea we wanted to hook up some telephones, and we got two tin cans and punched a hole in the bottom of the cans and took a long string and tied a knot on each end so that it didn't come through the can where the hole was. We could talk. It worked. We went from my house to his house with a long string with the two cans. You had to stretch it out. By golly, it did work.

During the summer, we looked forward to the firefighters setting up a sprinkler made of a long steel pipe on a tripod. Holes were bored down the one side, and a two-and-one-half-inch hose was hooked up to a fire hydrant to provide the spray. The cool water felt good on a hot summer day.

I remember that entertainment for our family changed considerably late in the 1930s when Joe bought a radio, and we spent our early evenings listening to serial programs, sometimes the news. On December 7, 1941, we were all glued to the radio listening to what was happening after the Japanese bombed Pearl Harbor. Our concern was for my brother Clyde, who was stationed in the U.S. Army there at the time.

HARRY JR.: When and how did you get your first bike?

HARRY SR.: I can't remember from whom I got it, but I think it was probably Lew who gave it to me. I do remember that he was very industrious and had a business venture selling potato chips and pretzels door to door to residents on a route in Tharptown. I think he had made enough money to buy a small car with a rumble seat not long after he turned 16. I may have been in the seventh or eighth grade when I got the bike, and I remember using it to pedal down to the Bowl-Mor with three other boys to set up pins.

Sometime before that, I had a scooter with two balloon tires found at the garbage dump that was once located at Weigh Scales. The scooter had a seat that you could put up or down. Another form of transportation that I used around the area near my home was something I made out of a discarded soda bottle case and a two-by-four on which parts of old roller skates were attached on the front and back.

HARRY JR.: You joined Boy Scouts as a young boy. Tell me about your experiences. What other groups did you join?

HARRY SR.: I was a Boy Scout with a troop that may have been the first established in Tharptown. I can't remember all the details, but I

Harry Deitz as a Boy Scout.

think my brother Clyde had something to do with its organization only a short time before he enlisted in the Army. I left the original troop for a while when I had small jobs helping Lew at a bakery and later dipping ice cream at Martz's Dairy Store. When war broke out, I rejoined the troop and earned the rank of first-class scout.

I remember some small details of Bags Woodley and me serving as messengers during blackouts and also being an airplane spotter on the roof of the American Legion Building in Shamokin during a civilian defense program organized by the Civil Air Patrol.

I don't remember it clearly, but they tell me I'm on a picture of members of a rifle club formed at Coal Township High School around 1942.

HARRY JR.: Did you get in trouble as a child?

HARRY SR.: In my younger years, I was very mischievous and probably was considered a brat by many of the well-to-do families in Tharptown. But I wasn't the only one.

Older boys were notorious for bullying the younger ones. That was the way it was back then. Once, we had a softball game going on at a field behind a red barn on Lott Street. Two of the Woodley boys, Jim, older brother of Bags, and Norm, got into an argument. Jim was holding the softball, and Norm, seeking possession of the softball, came after Jim, ready for a fight. Jim didn't know what to do, so he threw the ball to me. You know what happened next. Norm came after me, but I had an advantage. I ran faster than him, and by the time I got to the next street corner, I got rid of the softball, tossing it back to Jim.

One summer, I suffered a fracture of my left arm when I was swinging on a roof edge of a garage across the unpaved street between our house and the hill beyond the Reading Railroad tracks. Leo Fisher was with me at the time, and he ran home real fast because he was afraid he would get blamed for what happened to me.

Sometime earlier, I remember one particular day when the weather was warm, I decided that I didn't want to go to school, so I played hooky by hiding in a wooden box next to a property near our house. My sister caught me and paraded me back to the school, and I faced embarrassment as I walked back into the classroom.

Another time, Duke and I were scrounging through wastebasket refuse on a dumping site behind the Union Fire Company. Both of us were teenage smokers that our parents were unaware of. I picked up a cigarette butt that was only partially used and stuck the end in my mouth while I continued to search through the waste on the creek bank. Only minutes later, my dad, who spent most of his time at the hosey, came around the corner and saw me with that partially smoked cigarette in my mouth. He didn't say a word, just pointed toward our home, and I got the message. I hurried home, and he was only two or three steps behind me. Mom was in the kitchen when both of us arrived. I thought I could escape by running up the steps to the second floor. He took off his belt, and I got two licks before I was able to crawl under a buffet, one of two pieces of furniture in the room. By that time, mom came up the stairs and defended me by telling him my brother Clyde was responsible for me smoking because he had given me cigarettes.

Another time, I went to a grocery store with Duke and saw a basket full of wrapped peanut butter candy in front of a glass-enclosed display case. I thought no one would see me, so I stooped down and picked up two of them, placing them in my back pocket. I didn't realize that the owner was behind the glass case and could see everything in front of it.

There were several other similar incidents, but they were part of growing up in poverty. That meant not having the financial means of keeping up with other kids my age who seemed well off and had everything they wanted or needed.

We raised chickens all year round, and we had a chicken coop in the middle of the yard, right down close to where the outhouse was. We had one rooster, and he was vicious. If you went into that chicken house, he'd come after you. I left Dukey go in it one day, and I wouldn't let him out. The chicken came after him. God bless him.

HARRY JR.: I remember hearing about you being hit by a car or truck and seriously injured as a child. Tell me about that.

HARRY SR.: While growing up, there were good things and bad things. Some of them I remember. Some I don't.

At a young age, I was told I suffered a serious head injury when I fell while hanging on the back gate of a truck, picking up scrap not far from home. Family members told me I was taken to the hospital and treated in the emergency room. I don't know why I would have held on the back of the scrap truck and then panicked when it started to pick up speed. But that incident was one I heard about many times from family members and even others who knew my family at the time. I survived, thank God, or I wouldn't be writing this.

HARRY JR.: *The most serious injury our father suffered was on the morning of September 26, 1931, when he was three years old and after the family had moved to Tharptown. According to a front-page story in the* Shamokin News-Dispatch *that day, he walked onto the highway near his home and was hit by a car. He was listed in critical condition in the Shamokin State Hospital with "contusions of the head and possible internal injuries." The lead of the story, which incorrectly listed him as Harry Jr., stated he "may not recover" from the injuries.*

BOY IS NEAR DEATH RESULT OF BEING RUN DOWN BY AUTO

Little son of Harry Deitz of Tharptown in Critical Condition in Hospital From Injuries Received in Accident This Morning

Three-year-old Harry Deitz, Jr., the son of Harry Deitz, Sr., Tharptown miner, may not recover from injuries sustained when he walked into the state highway and was struck by an automobile near his home this morning.

An examination at the Shamokin State Hospital, where the child was taken soon after the accident, revealed that he sustained contusions of the head and possibly internal injuries. Dr. George W. Reese, superintendent at the hospital, said it was impossible to determine the exact extent of the child's injuries before 24 hours.

Jack C. Winters, 20, of 231 Water street, Northumberland, a former Northumberland high school athlete, was the driver of the automobile.

The accident occurred at the intersection in front of the Tharptown state police sub-station about 9:15 o'clock. State troopers immediately took charge of the case and questioned Winters.

The automobile driven by the youth was a Dodge coupe belonging to William W. VanAlen, of Front street, Northumberland. Winters said he was employed by VanAlen, and was authorized to operate the machine.

Winters told the state police that he was driving toward Shamokin at a speed of about 15 miles per hour when the child suddenly came out of the side street. Winters said he made a desperate effort to stop the car before it struck the child.

The mother of the injured child was so grief-stricken that she could hardly recall the boy's name when questioned shortly after the probably-fatal mishap.

Winters was graduated from Northumberland high school in 1929. He participated in other scholastic activities at the high school in addition to sports, and is well known in his home town.

Deitz is employed at the Cameron colliery.

BOY WHO WAS HIT BY AUTO RECOVERING

Harry Deitz, 3, of Tharptown, Victim of Accident Near Home Saturday, Removed from Hospital to Home of Parents

Three-year-old Harry Deitz has sufficiently recovered from injuries sustained in a motor accident Saturday morning to permit his removal from the Shamokin State Hospital to his home in Tharptown. The boy was removed to his home Sunday, after being held under observation at the hospital for more than 24 hours.

The boy, who is the son of Mr. and Mrs. Harry Deitz, Sr., was first thought to have received internal injuries, in addition to cuts about the head, but none was discovered during his stay at the hospital. Hospital attendants feared that he had received internal injuries which might prove fatal, but their fears were alleviated when the child showed signs of recovering.

Jack C. Winters, 20, of Northumberland, the driver of the coupe which struck the boy when he ran into the street at the intersection near the Tharptown state police sub-station, was released after he made a written report of the accident and was questioned by state police.

Stories from *Shamokin News-Dispatch*: Page 1 on September 26, 1931 (left) and Page 2 on September 28.

According to the paper, "The mother of the injured child was so grief-stricken that she could hardly recall the boy's name when questioned shortly after the probably fatal mishap."

Two days later, a story on Page 2 reported that he had been released from the hospital after it was determined there were no internal injuries.

It's not entirely clear if those two accounts—falling off the truck and being hit by the car—were the same incident and that details of the stories told by family members changed years later. Dad was too young to remember being injured, and no one else in the family clarified it while they were alive.

What do you know about your grandparents?

HARRY SR.: Both my paternal grandparents and my maternal grandfather died before I was born, but I do remember my maternal grandmother. Her name was Rose Sunbury, and she came to America (from Austria) and joined her husband, Anthony, in running the farm at Shamrock. I think it was not long after her husband died in 1927, she went to live with an older daughter, Mary Smith, a nurse, who resided in the Boston area. I believe she came to live with us sometime around 1935. I remember she could barely speak English, and she and my mom talked to each other in German most of the time.

Grandmother Sunbury and I were close. She had a friend who lived in Ranshaw. Grandmother Sunbury liked to have a little nip once in a while. One time I remember her taking me with her on the trolley to visit her friend in Ranshaw. It was my first trolley ride, and I was very excited as any youngster would be. When we got to Ranshaw, one of the first things grandmother's friend offered was a nip of the hard stuff. Grandmother thought it would be funny, so she offered me a taste too. Well, it wasn't funny to me. I made faces, spit the stuff out, and from that time on, I never liked whiskey.

I remember the night (June 1, 1938) that Grandmother Sunbury died, climaxing a long battle with cancer. The funeral was held several days later in our house. I was in the fourth grade at the time, and as was the custom, I stayed home from school on the day of the funeral. It was in June, only a few days until the end of the school year, and it shattered my record of perfect attendance.

Rosalee Sunbury and daughter Christine, circa 1920s.

I'm told that Grandmother Sarah Starr Deitz also had come to live with my parents in the home on Oak Street, where she died. Grandmother Sunbury was buried aside of her husband in St. Edward Cemetery in Springfield. Grandmother Deitz was buried in Shamokin Cemetery.

HARRY JR.: *Dad's paternal grandfather, Karl Maximillian Deitz, was born around 1845 in Germany and died around 1887 possibly in Washington, D.C. His paternal grandmother, Sarah Ann (Starr) Deitz, was born in 1840 in Llewellyn, Pa., and died in 1927 in Coal Township. His maternal grandfather, Anthony Sunbury, was born in 1863 in Austria and died in 1927 in Watertown, Mass. His maternal grandmother, Rosalee (Pesanka) Sunbury, was born in 1861 in Austria and died in 1938 in Coal Township.*

Tell me what you remember about the lives of each of your siblings— when they were born, their personalities, how well they did in school, sports and activities, what they did for a living.

HARRY SR.: **Dave (1914-2001, age 86):** Dave was a handsome young man and always was very reserved. He was industrious, always looking for some way to get money. With a friend named Fred Munson, he decided to mine coal, and the two of them constructed a makeshift, manually operated breaker out of used lumber in an area west of our home in Tharptown. They processed only one or two loads of coal and decided the time involved was not worth the effort. The project was abandoned.

Dave

Dave was a good vocalist in Coal Township High School's chorus and played football for the Purple Demons. But during his junior year, he quit school to help with the family's finances after Dad was hurt in the mines. I remember that Dave had several health issues during his early teens, including pneumonia.

His good looks got him in trouble, and at an early age, he had to get married to a girl named Natalie Laux. Dave never smoked. He signed up for the draft at the outset of World War II but was not accepted, I think because of some health problem, and he was married and had a son named David. Of the five boys in the family, he was the only one who did not serve in the military, but he did contribute by working for many years at the Middletown Air Depot. His life was devoted to being a businessman in Steelton (owning a taxicab company). He died of a stroke.

Clyde (1916-1979, age 62): Clyde was the picture image of my dad. He had the nickname "Tarzan" because he was the adventurous one, very athletic, and interested in boxing, for which he earned many honors while serving in the Army, including a tour of duty in Hawaii during the bombing by the Japanese on December 7, 1941. He entered the service late in the 1930s, and that tour of duty included being wounded in action during a skirmish somewhere in the Philippines. I think it was Guam.

He played baseball with a team in the West Branch League representing Uniontown, sponsored by Union Fire Company and coached by a teacher named Victor Carter. It was sort of an offshoot semipro team composed of guys from the immediate area, including Shamokin, who

had some talent as baseball players. I can't
remember it all, but something concerning
Clyde involved him in some trouble. He
had an interest in stalking and trapping wild
animals, including polecats. He was married
while serving in the army, but it didn't last
long. Clyde was a heavy smoker during his
youth and army career.

Clyde

His lack of education didn't help him
land a good job, even after he was married.
His career was centered on being a butcher
for Shamokin Packing Company, one of the
few industries that employed men of Tharptown and surrounding areas
during the depression and years to follow. Clyde married a single mother
named Nellie Stepp and was the only one of the family besides me who
remained in the Shamokin area to work and raise a family.

Quilla Mae (1919-1989, age 70): Like Dave and Clyde, she didn't
stay in school long after the eighth grade. I can't recall too much of her life
during the early years. I remember that before 1928, there was a two-story
elementary school on the corner of what is now Center and 14th Streets
in the center of Tharptown. It was a large building, and my sister took me
there to see a play presented by the students and in which she had a role.
There were iron fire escapes on both sides of the building. A room on the
second floor was utilized as an auditorium on the south side of the brick
building. It was where the students held entertainment programs.

Quilla, who was named after a nurse who worked for Dr. Ben Bealor,
our family doctor, apparently was very active in school groups, but when
she left school at a very early age, she worked for an itinerant carnival as
a lady with four legs, created by an illusion using mirrors. The circus was
playing up in Mt. Carmel, and we went to see her. It was Joe and mom
and me. She was there, and I said, "My sister doesn't have four legs." And
everybody looked at me. I was very young. I think maybe in the first or
second grade of school.

She got into some kind of trouble for which she spent time in cus-
tody of the county. It was there she met her first husband, Foster Watts,

who drove a tractor-trailer for a firm selling coal to residents of Baltimore. While living in Baltimore, she worked at a restaurant as a waitress. When they returned to Shamokin, they adopted a little girl and named her Nancy. Quilla and her husband later lived in two rooms of the house in Tharptown, where mom and dad and the siblings, along with Joe Bray, lived. Quilla's life was marked by hardships after her husband died of a stroke and her daughter married.

Quilla Mae

But she had many good traits and for years lived alone, worked for a retail outlet, and was well-liked in the business community and throughout the community in which she had many close friends. Later in life, she met Jack Dean, an auto transmission repairman dealer and stamp collector. They were happily married and lived in Shamokin for many years until she died of colon cancer in the late 1980s.

Ben (1921-2014, age 92): There is no question that Benjamin Franklin Deitz was the most ambitious and the smartest son of Harry and Christine Deitz in Tharptown. Had he finished one more year as a student at Coal Township High School, he certainly would have been among the top honor students in his graduating class. But, like the older three siblings, he needed to help with the family's financial problems by going to work. To that end, he left school at the end of his junior year to join what was then known as the Civilian Conservation Corps that the federal government organized during the Great Depression. He spent the summer at the CCC Camp at Masten in the northernmost section of Pennsylvania.

When the end of summer approached, he changed his mind about going back to school, so he enlisted in the Army when his brother Clyde reenlisted. During basic training at a fort in South Carolina, he met and married a southern belle named Bernice Brazell Plylor and then became the father of a baby girl just months before he was shipped to the United Kingdom for duty in the European Theater at the height of the war on

that side of the world. Ben attained the rank
of Master Sergeant. His marriage to Bernice
ended in divorce following the war when he
returned to Shamokin and got work as a coal
miner, and his ex-wife opted to stay in her
native community of Winnsboro, S.C.

Ben later obtained employment as a tech-
nician at the Sylvania plant in York, Pa. In the
meantime, he met and later married Harriet
Woodley and became the father of two more
daughters before that union was dissolved.
Ben died several years ago, and his remains   Ben
were interred at Indiantown Gap National Cemetery.

Lew (1924-1984, age 59): Lewis Henry Deitz followed in the footsteps of four older siblings by leaving school before completing his junior
year to work in a bakery. Even at a young age, he had the knowledge
and ambition to become a retailer. He proved this before he left school
when he organized and operated a self-sustaining pretzel and potato chip
program to obtain spending money, buying quantities at wholesale prices
and then selling combined packages door-to-door at a profit. It was a
success. He not only earned enough money to buy a small car with a
rumble seat, but he became instant friends of many people in Tharptown
and Shamokin, including state highway patrolmen who were quartered

in a former dwelling in the community and
a schoolteacher and his family that took a
special liking of him to the extent that they
arranged and paid for a trip to Wills Eye
Hospital in Philadelphia to correct what at
the time was called cross-eyes.

In addition to being popular in the community, Lewis had another asset. He was a
talented musician, playing trumpet with the
high school band, and he later organized
bands hired for dance and other entertainment programs in the area. While the war   Lew

was still on in the middle 1940s, Lew couldn't escape the draft. After basics, he was assigned to a quartermaster division in the U.S. Army in New Jersey, where he met and married a lovely young and divorced lady named Audrey Morris, a mother with two children. They had a daughter of their own when they lived in Trevorton, Pa., where Lew was employed as a clerk for a large coal sales company. Later, Lewis put his business ambitions to work by opening a successful appliance sales and repair store in Pompano Beach, Florida. Lew died of cancer in 1984.

2

Determined to Escape Poverty

As he entered his teens, the path that lay before our father was predictable and uninspiring. The 1940s brought more change for the nation, which continued its slow recovery from the Great Depression and faced new challenges with its involvement in World War II.

The Deitz family's circumstances hadn't improved when our father started his freshman year at Coal Township High School in the fall of 1942. Poverty was all he knew during the early part of his life, and by now, he began to feel the effects of his family's struggles and anticipate a dim future for himself.

One by one, his four brothers and sister quit school to find work to help support the family. He did, also. Twice. But there was something embedded in him that made him understand the value of education. Why and where it came from is hard to pinpoint. But he did return and graduate from high school—the first in his family to do so.

Three of his brothers would eventually build comfortable lifestyles, but they left the area to do it—Dave to Steelton, Ben to York, Lew to Pompano, Florida. Our father was determined to remain near home and make something of himself. But for that to happen, he had to go halfway around the world for a brief time.

Even when World War II was nearing an end, our father saw the army as a possible step forward. He not only could earn money to send home to help support his parents, but he also would acquire knowledge and skills as a photographer, which would set him on a promising career path.

There was another reason he needed to find a solution out of his life of poverty. On April 6, 1946, he met Beverly Jane Smith, a 15-year-old, dark-haired beauty from Shamokin. It was love at first sight for both of them. But he quickly realized how his limited resources and prospects for meaningful employment could affect any potential future they might have together. He was embarrassed by his shabby clothes and lack of spending money. He needed to know—and for her to know—that he could provide a comfortable lifestyle for them.

So two months after they met, he went to see her and told her he had joined the army. He remembers the sadness they shared that night. But it was a sacrifice and investment that would pay dividends for the rest of his life and for the life they would build together.

HARRY JR.: Tell me about attending high school. Were you nervous when you started? What was your favorite subject in school? In what activities or sports were you involved? Who were your friends?

HARRY SR.: With eighth-grade graduation finished, including getting all dressed up for a class photo, I looked forward during the late summer of 1942 to the opening of classes at Coal Township High School.

I think all the boys my age were glad for the start of school because the summer had been extremely busy with activities and responsibilities dedicated to a home-front effort for the war that was escalating. Clyde and Ben were already in the military, and Lewis was rapidly approaching the age when he would join them. Lewis and I were involved with the war effort during home-front activities that included soliciting funds for an honor roll of the names of all the young men from Tharptown serving in the military. The honor roll was erected and dedicated on the lawn in front of the grammar school during the early years of World War II.

I was excited about the approach of the new school term in a new environment and participating in new programs, classes, and activities, including volleyball and football and various studies, some of which were very new to me. I rode a school bus to the high school, located about two miles from the center of Tharptown. As freshmen in the west end of the district, we were assigned classes in two separate buildings—the old Garfield elementary school on West Chestnut Street in the morning and the main high school on Juniper Street in the afternoon. When our

The 1942 8th grade graduation class at the Uniontown School. Harry Deitz, second from right in the front row (and in the blowup on the facing page), explains how he looked so well dressed: "Mom had been saving for it, and Joe helped, and I had a couple pennies I got from somebody. I got those shoes when a little boy who lived in the town got sick and died, and they needed eight from the class to be pallbearers. I was picked to be one of the pallbearers. So somehow mom bought me the shoes then. That is not a matching suit. It's a pair of trousers and a jacket. They were used. Anything I ever got was used."

school bus arrived at the high school in the morning, we had to walk three blocks to the Garfield for the morning sessions, then walk back to the high school building for the afternoon classes.

Among the classes I liked that first year in high school were Algebra, taught by Daniel Kwasnoski, and history, taught by Martin Gricoski, in the Garfield building.

One of my best friends, Duke Culton, didn't join Bags Woodley and me there because his family had moved from Tharptown to the Springfield section, where separate freshmen and sophomore classes were held for two years in the old Pulaski High School building. Duke's family later returned to Tharptown.

Bags and I went out for the football team as freshmen, but we didn't like the grueling practices on a rocky field on the hill behind the high school, so we turned in our uniforms several weeks after practice started.

One of my friends in the freshman class was Joe Snyder, who resided along the road leading from the center of Tharptown to what was then known as the State Hospital for Miners and Their Families. It was Joe, whom I joined at Martz's Dairy Store on West Arch Street, dipping ice cream during the evenings. Joe also was my mentor when I learned to drive. He accompanied me to Sunbury when I turned 16 and took my state driver's license test in 1944.

One other friend in high was Jack Paretti, another Tharptown native, who left school as a sophomore to join the Merchant Marines. I wanted to go into that group with him, but I was two pounds under the minimum requirement of 130 pounds.

HARRY JR.: You were the first in your family to graduate from high school, but you quit twice and returned both times. Why did you quit in ninth grade, and why did you go back?

HARRY SR.: While many of my fellow students in high school didn't have any worries about their financial survival even during hard times when the nation was in the midst of World War II, it was evident by the used clothing I wore, the need at times of a haircut, and my slim physical appearance that may have been the result of poor nutrition, that my family was still struggling with poverty. My contributions to fundraising efforts by individual classes to help the home-front war effort by purchasing war bonds and stamps, care packages, and holiday gifts for servicemen representing the community never exceeded 25 cents. Admittedly, I was embarrassed more than once.

At the same time, I worked at night at Martz's dipping ice cream or making milk shakes until an 11 o'clock closing time, and then rode my bicycle two miles to the Bon Ton Bakery in the upper end of Tharptown

to help my brother, Lew, slice and wrap fresh-baked bread for delivery
to retail grocery stores. Our work would wind up between 1 and 2 a.m.
each morning. Lew rewarded me with a small amount from his meager
salary. Part of what we earned helped the family's financial situation,
augmenting what mom got for scrubbing floors and washing clothes of
neighbors and others. It was barely enough to purchase food and pay bills
for coal, electricity, water, and other essentials.

I managed to keep working one job, helping at another, and then going to school five days a week. It continued at that pace until Lew got his
draft notice and became the third member of the family to enter the U.S.
Army. In the meantime, I was offered a full-time job to help a beverage
dealer deliver products to bars and restaurants in the area. It meant that I
had to quit school, a little over two months shy of the school year's end.

But things brightened up in the months to follow. Lew's entry into
the military resulted in an allotment for my parents, and Joe got a steady
job at a new coal processing plant one block east of our home. In addition, two elderly people rented rooms in our large house. With the
turn of events, I was able to return to school the following September. It
meant that I would need to repeat the first year as a freshman. It was a
fresh ray of sunshine on a cloudy day. I continued to work at Martz's with
Joe Snyder for several months after my return to school.

Harry Jr.: Who was your first girlfriend?

Harry Sr.: Mom (Beverly) was it. She was my one and only.

I didn't have any girlfriends. We used to get together at the Bogetti
house on their porch. A couple had paired off with boy and girlfriends,
but there was somebody else besides me that we didn't have a girlfriend.

There was a girl named Joan, and I went out on a date with her one
time. That was the first girl I kissed. We went with her sister and her sister's boyfriend. The sister's boyfriend had a car, and we went to the movies.

There were a couple of girls that I talked to, but there was nothing
serious.

HARRY JR.: How and when did you meet Beverly?

HARRY SR.: It was April 6, 1946, at the Roaring Creek watershed.
She was on a picnic with the girls from her class. There were five or six
of them. They had a wiener roast. A friend and I walked through the

watershed and looked for a dog that the friend had and got lost. It was a warm day, and we went by the sand spring, got a drink, and came down this path, and here were these girls. That's when I met her.

HARRY JR.: What attracted you to her?

HARRY SR.: I thought she was a good-looking girl. Very beautiful. She had black hair, and she was wearing slacks. I had a jacket on that my brother Ben had left at home when he went to the service. When he returned from the service, it had a ruptured duck pin on it that they gave to the servicemen when honorably discharged. I wore that, and she was cold, so I gave her my jacket to keep warm.

It was love at first sight.

She gave me her telephone number, and that night I stopped at the gas station where Harry Brosius was and where we gathered in the middle of Tharptown. There was a pay phone, and I told Harry about the nice girl I met at the water company, and I said I'd like to see her. He said, "Why don't you take the car." He had a '46 Mercury.

I met her on a Sunday, and the next day I called her, and her mother answered the phone. I asked if Beverly was there, and she put Beverly on. I told her, "Would you mind if I come up to see you?" She said, "Come up and meet my parents." I took Harry's car and went up.

I met her mom, who was ironing clothes in the kitchen. Her mom was really cool.

HARRY JR.: Where was your first date? How often did you see her in the beginning?

HARRY JR.: I asked her if she'd like to go to the movies some night. I think it was that Friday night we went to the movies. We sat on the balcony up on the left side of the Victoria Theater. The movie was *Sentimental Journey*, and that was our theme song.

We'd get together Friday and Saturday. She had a girlfriend named Betty, who had a boyfriend, and he had a car with a rumble seat. We got together with them quite a few times. The funny part about it is that the gas stations were giving out favors when you bought gas. They gave you knives and forks and spoons or crystal ware if you got gas. If you went to the movies on certain nights, they also gave you some of that stuff. We started collecting it. We didn't even know we were going to get married.

Our mother and father on April 6, 1946, the day they met.
Apparently one of her girlfriends had a camera and took several
pictures of them with her wearing his jacket because she was
cold. Our father says, "It was love at first sight."

We went out to the movies, and she liked to go to Arvey's Restaurant.
It was right across the street from where the Victoria was. Her favorite
was a BLT—bacon, lettuce, and tomato sandwich. I borrowed enough
money from Harry to take her to the movies and take her to the restaurant a couple of times. He kept a tab and said whenever you get any
money, you can pay your bill.

It got to a point where I owed Harry Brosius quite a bit of money. I
couldn't go out very often because I didn't have the money. What little I
had was what Harry gave me for helping him at the gas station or doing
some odd jobs around the neighborhood.

I'd go up to her house, and we'd sit in the parlor and maybe listen to the radio. Her mom and dad would go to bed. I would ride the bus up. It cost ten cents. I'd go up once or twice a week. We went to (Trinity Lutheran) Church a couple of times together, over on Sunbury Street. Dr. Fry was the pastor. They had Luther League on a Thursday night, and they had choir practice on a Thursday night. I sat in with the choir a couple of times and sang with her.

HARRY JR.: How did you get along with her parents? Did they accept you? She was only 15 when you met, and you were almost 18. Was that an issue for them?

HARRY SR.: They were nice. They had certain rules by which we had to abide. I was 17. Both of us were young.

When I'd go up to see her, at 11 o'clock sharp, her mom would come to the top of the steps and say, "Beverly, tell your friend it's time to go home." That went on like that until the middle of June.

The big thing was I couldn't afford to do the things I would have liked to have done to win her attention. I really didn't have to because we were both satisfied to be with each other. She was beautiful. It was love at first sight.

HARRY JR.: With this new relationship, why did you suddenly decide to leave school and join the army?

HARRY SR.: At the end of May or the beginning of June, they had the junior class prom at Coal Township. Being in the junior class, I was able to take somebody. So I asked her if she'd like to go to the dance at the American Legion. There was no charge for it. I borrowed $2 from Harry to put on my tab. She wore a gown, and we went to the dance at the Legion.

Across the street, there was an arcade. We went out to eat and went to this arcade and had a picture taken. They had one of those positive-print machines. I had one of her by herself. I felt bad because I wore a suit that my brother bought when he returned from the service. It was too big for me. He lent me his shirt and tie and a suit, and a pair of shoes. And I felt bad because it didn't fit. Everything was baggy. I just felt bad. I couldn't get a job because the war was over and jobs were hard to find, any kind of job. I wanted to do things, and I couldn't do things.

In the middle of June, I was at Harry's gas station, and another guy from Tharptown named Tom Carr came into the gas station. He said:

"Harry, I just signed up for the army. Why don't you go with me?" I don't know what made me think about it. They required a test to get your IQ. We went up together, and I was thinking all the time I'm embarrassed to go out with her. I don't have good clothes to wear. I needed a haircut. It was awful. That embarrassment caused me to think if I went to service, I'd have some decent clothes to wear and have some money.

I figured it was the answer to my problem. I just was ashamed. Not to be with her, but what I had to wear. I couldn't depend on my mom for anything or my dad. I owed so much money to Harry. I think I owed him about $12 or $14. That was a lot.

Tom talked me into going up and talking to the recruiting officer. He gave me a spiel and said servicemen got $21 per month, and they just raised it to $50 per month. That's over $10 a week and all your clothes and food.

I took the test and came out with a score of 130, which they said was pretty darn good. The guy said I'd do all right in the army. I said OK.

HARRY JR.: How did mom react when you told her you were joining the army?

HARRY SR.: I went up that night, and I told Beverly I was going for my test in Harrisburg the next day. Her mom came to the steps at 11 o'clock and said, "Beverly, tell your friend to go home." Beverly said, "Mom, I'm going to stay up with him a little while because he's going to the army tomorrow." She didn't give us a hard time.

Beverly wasn't mad. I told her, "I can't do the things I want to do for you." I said: "If I go to the service, I can learn a trade. I'll come back, and we can pick up from here if you want. We can write to each other every day." She finally said OK.

I told her: "You don't need to be pinned down. You can do what you want. You can go out with somebody. Fine."

I went home, went to bed, got up at seven, and went to Harrisburg with Tom.

HARRY JR.: Tell me about joining the Army. Where were you trained and stationed?

HARRY SR.: There were 26 guys on the bus. We went to Harrisburg, and to be truthful, I didn't think I was going to pass the physical. I weighed 130 pounds. I had been turned down for the Merchant Marines because I didn't even weigh 130 pounds.

I passed the physical with flying colors. So did Tom, and so did most of the 26 guys on the bus. Next thing you know, we're in the auditorium, raising our right hand and saying we swear to uphold the Constitution of the United States. Then we're on a troop train to the induction center at Fort Meade in Maryland.

We walked into this big auditorium. And one of the COs welcomed us. We had the night off, and the USO had a dance in a rec hall. There were a lot of girls there. I felt I didn't want to be bothered. I felt I had a friend at home. I couldn't say she was my girlfriend, but I had a friend at home.

The next couple of days were getting indoctrinated into Army life. We got our shots the next morning. We sat in the barber's chair, and they cut all our hair off. We got our uniforms. They gave us another complete physical. We packed our civilian clothes in boxes and sent them home. I heard that my mom cried when she got the box.

We were there three or four days, then we boarded a train and went from Maryland to Fort McClellan, Alabama. That took two days. All the way down, I had tears in my eyes. I kept saying to myself: "What did I do? What did I do? What did I do?"

I felt bad that I didn't see Beverly. I was homesick the first couple of days. We got to Fort McClellan and got off the train, and there was a big sign in the amphitheater that said, "Kill or be killed." That sent chills up and down your back.

The barracks were nothing more than one-story huts. There were six bunks in each hut, and we were assigned alphabetically to the huts. The next couple of days was all indoctrination. We got a rifle issued to us. We went to classes. We were assigned different sections of the 20th Infantry Division. I was in Squad C.

The next morning we were out doing a quarter-mile run, then the next day we went to a half, then three-quarters, then a full mile. We had everything, all the infantry training, from learning how to fire an M-1, how to take an M-1 apart and put it back together and keep it clean. We did close-order drilling. We went on hikes and out to the rifle range once or twice a week.

Dad with mom's photo during his military time in Japan. He sent the one below to her with the message: "to Bev. the sweetest girl in the world. All my Love. Harry"

One of the days, they took a group picture. I didn't get on the group picture because I was assigned to go to the dentist. They pulled about four teeth. They were all bad. I didn't take care of them.

While I was in basic training, the first week was bad. I felt like I made a mistake. I missed her something terrible. I knew I liked her. My feelings were that I really loved her from the beginning.

My first week in basic training was really bad because it seemed like everybody was getting letters and packages the first couple of days. I waited and waited, and on the sixth day, I got a letter. But I had to write to her first and give her my address.

I got my first letter from her, and aah, she said she missed me but was spending a lot of time down at the cottage. Her dad and mom owned a cottage at Happy Hollow. She spent time down there at the swimming pool. She had some friends. She was dating while I was in the service.

They had things that you never forgot. When we first got there, to Fort McClellan, there was a kid in the outfit named Kapps. When we were in the amphitheater, he stood up, and he hollered to the general: "I'm homesick. I want to go home." Well, for the next two or three weeks, he never forgot that because they had him doing everything. They had him washing the barracks floor. They had him doing KP. I struck it rich. They called the guys out for KP by the alphabet. The first couple was ABC, and they stopped at C. Then they had KP and guard duty. When it was my turn, they skipped me and went from D to E.

After basic training, they assigned you where you would go, either to the East Coast or the West Coast for debarkation. Quite a few of us went back home on the train, and I spent 14 days on what was called a delay en route. It wasn't a furlough.

HARRY JR.: On those 14 days delay en route, did you see mom?

HARRY SR.: We spent the whole 14 days together. It was harvest time, and her dad took us to different places to pick up produce.

When I was home, I was able to pay Harry back. He lent me a car, so I could go up and talk to Bev, and we could go to the movies.

We'd walk from Eighth Street down to the movies. And we'd always go to Arvey's Restaurant after the movies.

When I went back from my delay en route, I didn't contact Beverly for 14 days at sea and ten days at Fort McClellan. Until I sent her an airmail letter with my new address, I didn't contact her for four or five weeks. Then when the letters came in, it was every day. Every day. She would write me, and I would write her every day.

My mom or Joe sent me the newspaper every day in the mail. That helped me keep in touch with what was going on at home.

HARRY JR.: What did you do in the service? How did you get involved with photography?

HARRY SR.: That wasn't until I went overseas. I was strictly a rifleman until I got over at the Fourth Replacement Depot in Yokohama, Japan. I attribute the good luck I had with that to a guy at Camp Stoneman who interviewed me. When you went into the service, they filled out a thing called a Form 20, and it's what you did before you went into the service. My answer was "student."

I was to report out to Camp Stoneman in California on the 14th of September. When I was at Camp Stoneman, I credit a guy who interviewed me for the second time before I shipped out. He was a first sergeant, and he said, "It's not good that you have on your Form 20 that you were a student. Didn't you do anything else that we could put down? If we just put down student, when you get overseas, you're going to be in an infantry outfit, or you're going to be in some tank outfit. You're going to be in the big stuff. What else did you do?"

I said, "I drove tractor-trailer with my brother-in-law once in a while when he went to Baltimore and delivered coal, but it was only one summer."

He said, "Anything else?"

I said, "Yea, I fooled around a little with photography."

He said, "Did you have a camera?"

I said: "No, I didn't have a camera, but I learned how to do developing. I did it in the basement of our house for my aunt one time and my mom."

He said, "I'll put down that you were a hobbyist in photography."

I said, "OK."

I shipped out from San Francisco on the 26th of September. Was I sick! I don't think I was out past the Golden Gate Bridge more than three miles, and I was sick. I was on the third level. There were six bunks in the hold where we were quartered. The ship was called the Marine Adder, and it was a troop ship. It was very small and got tossed around in the waves. We hit a storm about three days out. I can always remember the captain saying: "Soldier, you got to eat. You got to eat."

When I got to the Fourth Replacement Depot, they looked at my form and said: "The engineer outfit photographer at Tokyo is being discharged. Let's send him up there." It was a stroke of luck. It was more than a stroke of luck. It was God's blessing. I don't know why God would want to bless me. I wasn't a steady churchgoer. I wasn't what you call a good Christian. But when I got to the Fourth Replacement Depot, they shipped me up to Tokyo.

The Japanese civilians there were experts in the field of photography, and I learned more from them than I would have from anybody else. I was their boss. We had a darkroom in the basement of our office building that was located only half a block from Tokyo Station. Our motor pool was right next door to the office building.

When I got to the 584th Engineer Construction Battalion, I went down in the basement. These two guys were so friendly. I told them I don't know too much. This one guy named Keenan—I never knew his first name—they showed me, and it didn't take me long to learn how to use a 4x5 camera. It was a Crown Graphic.[7] They taught me a lot.

HARRY JR.: Tell me about experimenting with photography when you were at home and before you joined the service.

HARRY SR.: Somebody gave me a Popular Science magazine. There was an article about how to process pictures. They built their own enlarger.

So I went up to Smink's store on Market Street, and the guy there kind of took a liking to me. He said, "Why didn't I just take a starter kit?" It cost just a couple of bucks. It was cheap. It was a kit on how to develop pictures. I bought a small pack of paper. One time my Aunt Em brought some negatives over and asked if I'd do them. I printed them between two pieces of glass. I'd expose it to the light and process the piece of paper, and let it dry in the sun. That's how I got started.

I didn't have money to continue that, but it was a start. I'm glad I did it because it opened the door to what would happen later in the service.

HARRY JR.: What kind of photography work did you do in Japan?

Dad using a 4x5 camera while in Japan and two portraits from the service.

HARRY SR.: Our engineer outfit was responsible for the planning for the rebuilding of the areas bombed out. And there were plenty of them. They also were responsible for building places where officers and their wives stayed, real nice housing projects. They were responsible for building some infrastructure, like the Tokyo airport called Haneda, the 20-mile road between Tokyo and Yokohama, and any big buildings. They were responsible for it. It was a regular construction battalion.

My job was to do progressive pictures on the projects. I could call the airport and take photos from the air. I took some photos of Mount Fuji. I did that maybe once a month. We'd go out to this housing project, and I'd climb up on top of the water tower with my friend from the dark room, and he and I would set up the camera on a tripod, and we'd take a series of shots for a panorama. We'd go back and print the pictures and paste them together. So the captain would have this big board with all these pictures and know when they were taken and the progress.

I got in good with the officers. My first sergeant was from Uniontown, Pennsylvania. He was my buddy. And there was another one named Tom O'Cleary, and he was a staff sergeant. He and I got to be friends, too.

The first month I was there, I wanted to see our inventory, how many supplies we were using, what equipment we had, and what equipment we might need. We never had an enlarger. We always used a box printer. I made a list of everything we had and everything we might need, and I gave it to the captain. I didn't expect it, and this was in November, but the next thing I knew, there was an order that came down, "Private Harry J. Deitz is hereby promoted to Tech T-5." Wow. All these guys were going from private to first-class private then to corporal, which was my equivalent, and here I went from private to corporal.

I was promoted again on May 22 to T-4. That was the equivalent of a sergeant.

HARRY JR.: When did you leave the service?

HARRY SR.: I never had a furlough. I enlisted on the 18th of June. I enlisted for 18 months. That was standard at the time of enlistment. That meant I would be discharged in December 1947. That's when my enlistment would be up. But I didn't have a furlough, so I had furlough time coming. That brought me back to the end of October.

HARRY JR.: What was it like when you returned home?

HARRY SR.: I flew back from San Francisco. I didn't want to come back on the train because it took three days, costing almost as much. I had $150 travel pay and back pay for two months, which was $125 a month, and I had furlough pay, which was another $125.

I went from San Francisco back to Pittsburgh. It took 19 hours. That was the first week in November. Then I took a train to Harrisburg, then another train to Sunbury. Then a bus to Shamokin. Mom didn't know I was coming home.

Quilla and her husband were living in two rooms in the house, and she had a telephone. I called her and told her I'm in Sunbury. She said, "Oh my God."

I said: "Don't tell mom. I should be there by 10 o'clock." At that time the bus service was pretty good.

I got off the bus at Sweitzer's bar with a carry suitcase. I opened the gate and started walking up the walk. Mom saw me, and she came running down the front yard. She gave me such a big hug and kiss. Dad, Joe, Quilla, Clyde, and Watsy were in the kitchen. They were all glad to see me. It was almost 16 months since I saw them. That was a long time.

HARRY JR.: Tell me what it was like when you went to see our mom?

HARRY SR.: When I docked at Camp Stoneman on the way back, they had a section you could go to and call home, and it was free. I called your mom, and I said, "Hi, honey, do you still love me?"

She didn't answer.

I said, "Let me hear you tell me you still love me."

She didn't answer. I thought maybe she doesn't love me anymore. I learned later her mom and dad were right there listening in on everything she was saying.

I'll never forget it. I got on the bus and got off at Chestnut Street, and I practically ran up that hill. Her mom was so glad to see me. She hugged me. Her dad came downstairs and shook hands with me. She was upstairs, and she came down. I looked at her, and I never saw anything so beautiful. She wouldn't hug me in front of her mom and dad. Anyhow, we made up for it later that night.

Her mom invited me to stay for dinner. We spent the afternoon together, and at night her mom and dad went to bed and left us alone.

I went home about 1 or 2 o'clock. I walked home. The next morning I got up, and sis and I went to the bank. While I was in the service, I sent her my monthly check because I didn't need any money. In addition to being a photographer, I worked at night and operated a 35mm simplex motion-picture machine at Tokyo Bowl. There were three of us that did that. I learned to do that and got extra money for that. I'd send that home, and Quilla would put that in an account. When I got home, I had over $500 in cash, and she had over $1,500 in that account. That $500 burned a hole in my pocket. I said the first thing we're going to do is buy clothes.

And I did at Sam Dluge's. I spent almost $200 on clothes. That was a lot at that time. I bought a brand-new, pin-stripe suit that your mother hated. Quilla loved it, though. She picked it out. I bought a topcoat. I never had a topcoat in my life. I bought two or three pairs of gabardine trousers, a pair of penny loafers, all new underwear and socks, a shirt, a leather jacket, and a couple of sweaters. I waited a long time for it.

HARRY JR.: Why did you decide to go back and graduate from high school?

HARRY SR.: I decided to go back to school when I was in Tokyo. I was very determined that I was going to finish high school. I decided I was going to go back and finish my senior year if I could. So I wrote a letter to Stanley Gililey, the high school principal, and I said I would like to come back and be the only member of my family to finish high school, and I'd like to be with the class of 1948 if at all possible. If not, I said, I'll wait till the class of 1949. That was early in the spring.

He wrote back and said, "Harry, we'll be glad to have you. As soon as you get back, come see me."

So Monday morning, after we went shopping, I walked out to the high school. I was still in uniform, went up to the office, and was welcomed like a lost sailor. That was early in November.

HARRY JR.: *It was unusual for someone in our father's situation to quit school two times, then return to school and graduate. The dropout rate was high. In his 1948 yearbook,* Le Souvenir, *there is an article on class history, and the decline in the class size because of dropouts each year is chronicled in detail. The freshman class that began with 266 students in 1944 had 166 graduates in 1948.*

Did you feel you fit in when you returned to school?

HARRY SR.: I did. The first couple of days were tough to get organized. The first class I went to was economics. I just walked in and introduced myself, and the teacher introduced me to the class. That's the way it was with all the other classes. I got involved with the journalism class. The teacher was Lewis Evans.

We had a teacher by the name of (Joseph) McCormick, and he was very patriotic. And the kids made fun of him because he was patriotic. He would have a class, and he would grab the American flag and squeeze it, and he'd say, "See how the blood comes out of this American flag? Harry knows what I'm talking about."

HARRY JR.: Did you play any sports or participate in other activities?

HARRY SR.: I was too old. If you were 19, you couldn't play sports. I was a member of the high school chorus that was taught by Gertrude Fisher. We would do musicals for the holidays. I participated in the gym classes, too.

I was a reporter for *The Clarion* (the monthly school newspaper), and I helped the guy taking pictures. I didn't take the pictures; that was his job. I advised him what to do. I had to do one article every month. The first month the article was a Christmas story. I wrote a fictitious story about a guy that was trimming a Christmas tree. He sat down, was tired, and fell asleep. While he slept, there was a short circuit, and the house caught fire. He kept hollering, "Fire." Here he was dreaming. He woke up and was so glad it was a dream. Everybody liked the story.

HARRY JR.: *During his senior year, our father was a member of the Glee Club, Operetta, and* Le Souvenir *yearbook staff. In the operetta,* Wild Rose, *a musical comedy, he played Theodore Willingham, a would-be poet. The brief poem under his yearbook picture was, "He is a boy with eyes of blue. Just watch out, he's taken too!"*

Did you attend your senior prom?

HARRY SR.: Beverly and I went to the prom, and it poured rain. I had a friend named Joan Dunkelberger. She and I were really good friends. Joan had a car she lent me. It was held at the legion. They had dinner and then a dance.

HARRY JR.: Did you attend your graduation ceremony?

Coal Township High School

This Certifies That

Harry J. Deitz

has completed the Course of Study prescribed by the Board of Education, for this High School, and is therefore entitled to this

Diploma

In Witness Whereof, we have hereunto affixed our signatures at Coal Township, Shamokin, Pennsylvania, this twenty-first day of June, A. D. 1948.

Dad's diploma, yearbook photo, and with some of the cast from the operetta "Wild Rose."

HARRY J. DEITZ
"Hamy"
429 Lott St.
ACADEMIC
Football 1, 2; Glee Club 4;
Press Club 4; Operetta 4;
LE SOUVENIR 4.
*He is a boy with eyes of blue
Just watch out, he's taken
    too!*

HARRY SR.: Yes, and so did mom and Beverly and Beverly's mom and dad. I think her mom and dad went to the operetta too.

At the same time, I got involved with Beverly at her church. I sang in the choir. I went to church almost every Sunday. And Luther League and choir practice. I had to either ride the bus or walk.

HARRY JR.: After graduation, what was your plan? Did you get a job?

HARRY SR.: I got paid for going to school under the G.I. Bill of Rights. They had a thing called the 52-20 club. You could sign up for 52 weeks and get $20 a week if you were in the service. It was like unemployment compensation.

And then I got a job at a furniture store. At that time, anything you got, you took. I was like a maintenance man. I swept the floors, repaired some furniture, and helped this guy deliver the furniture. He had a really expensive car. I used to take that down-home and wash it for him. I worked at that until one day, I went up to Beverly's, and her dad said: "Did you hear the news? Shroyers are going to start a newspaper."

HARRY JR.: Tell me how you got your first job in the newspaper business.

HARRY SR.: I owed the start of my career to my future father-in-law. At nighttime, I'd hop on the bus and go up and see Beverly. So this one time, I went up, and Beverly's dad said, "You're a professional photographer, right?"

I said, "I like to think I'm a professional photographer."

He belonged to the Masonic Lodge, and he said he was at the Masonic Lodge meeting, and Lawton Shroyer and John Shroyer were there, and they were giving a speech on planning to start a weekly newspaper in Shamokin. And he told me, "Why don't you go see them, and maybe you could get a job."

Shroyers sold dresses all over the nation. It was a good company. I went up to Shroyers the next morning. I talked to Lawton. I said, "Mr. Shroyer, I understand you might be starting a newspaper, and I thought maybe you could use a photographer. You know I was a photographer in WWII, and I'm well-acquainted with using a 4x5 camera."

He said, "Do you think you could get a 4x5 camera?"

I said, "I'll try. The good thing is that I'm under the G.I. Bill of Rights. They have a program that they will pay part of a person's salary for training." The salary was $40 a week. They paid $20, and the company paid $20.

This was January, and the paper wasn't going to come out till the spring. They introduced me to George Shroyer. He was a captain in the army. When I mentioned to him I was a photographer in the army, he hired me right away. He said, in the meantime, what was I going to do before the paper came out? They had set the date for May 16 for the first day of publication. They were going to buy a press and put it in this building on Shamokin Street.

He said: "Why don't you come to work at the dress factory and take pictures of the dress models? We'll send them out and see the styles." I used an old box camera. That's what I did until the first edition came out.

3

Driven to Succeed

For the first time, there were rays of hope in our father's life. He had returned from the service with a new skill. He graduated from high school. He was in love. And things soon would improve for him.

He was about to start a job that offered the possibility of a better future. Soon he would marry the beautiful young woman who had stolen his heart in the spring of 1946. They would buy their first house and start a family.

Our father had found an unexpected calling in the newspaper world, and from the beginning, he would develop a passion and obsession that would impact not only his career but also his family life.

His struggles weren't over. For most of his life, our father would fight a continual battle to get ahead. But he never gave up. In fact, each obstacle he faced seemed to make him more determined to be respected, needed, and successful.

That determination, however, came with a degree of self-protection and stubbornness, and he would lose the job where he had started his career over a matter of fairness and principle. That only served to make him more driven to prove himself and to become a better newsman. It would not be his last setback.

The experience he gained and the groundwork he laid during those early years of his career paved a path for him to move onto bigger and better things.

And he did.

HARRY JR.: When you landed your first newspaper job at the Shamokin Citizen, did you feel your future was more promising than at any time in your life to that point?

HARRY SR.: There are no words to describe the feeling I had when I emerged from the building on North Shamokin Street after meeting with John U. Shroyer and his sons, Lawton, John, George, and Barney. I wasn't overly religious, but as I now look back at it, I feel that God was with me because everything came together, and I was hired on the spot as a photographer for the planned weekly paper.

The opportunity to work at something I did while serving in the military was realized. That service time worked to Shroyers' advantage as well as mine because I convinced Mr. Shroyer and his sons that since the newspaper was a new adventure for them, my employment could be classified as "on the job training" under the G.I. Bill of Rights, which I had used to return to high school and which I still had quite a bit of entitlement.

The only problem was that our meeting was held in January, and the paper's debut wasn't scheduled until May or June. The question arose: "What work would I do until then?" George suggested using me to take photos during the interim of new dress styles manufactured in the plant on the hill overlooking Shamokin. So, the following Monday, I began my first full-time job in my life.

HARRY JR.: Tell me about the start of your newspaper career at the Citizen.

HARRY SR.: I kept doing dress pictures until they were ready to go. They didn't have all the stuff they needed. They needed a darkroom. They needed an enlarger. They had an office over in the back of the dress store on Market Street. There were three office partitions, and they took one section and made a darkroom.

The reporters would be at the office on Market Street. They'd write the copy and take it over to the building on Shamokin Street, and they'd set it up in type. They printed the paper with a flatbed press.

They hired two guys from Hazleton, Jerry Gallagher, and Al Steibing. Steibing was the advertising manager, and Gallagher was the editor. He was my first boss, and he was a nice guy. In the first edition, they had

The door at the right was the entrance to the first editorial office of the *Shamokin Citizen* on Market Street, behind Shroyers' dress store, beginning in 1949. The slot machine on the steps was used to raise money for the police retirement fund. The sign reads, in part: "If you must gamble play this slot machine and support a worthy cause. Entire proceeds will be given to the police retirement fund. Racketeers get no cut. Public accounting of income will be given weekly in *The Shamokin Citizen*." The picture was published in *Newsweek* magazine in 1950.

a story about a new plant coming to Paxinos. They scooped the *News-Dispatch* (the daily newspaper). It raised eyebrows. The first edition had a story about me being in the service as a photographer.

John U. Shroyer said, "Do you think you could take pictures of people and make them look good in the paper?" I said, "I'll try, sir." He said, "We're thinking about a column we'll call 'roving photographer.' " So I was out taking pictures of people, asking them a question and writing up their answers and using a little picture with them.

I consider the time I spent working for the weekly paper a learning experience that contributed to a long career as a news and commercial photographer, writer, and editor. The early years were difficult because of the adjustment in my home and work schedule, but the more I became

In the early 1950s, the *Shamokin Citizen* relocated to a new building on East Sunbury Street. *The Shamokin Citizen* continued to be published until 1967. The Shroyers Dress Company was closed in 1984.

involved, the more I enjoyed doing what I was hired to do. Taking photos of news events was demanding with no opportunity of "doing it over."

Initially, the working environment was not the best because our editorial staff was quartered behind a dress shop where the products manufactured at the Shamokin Dress Company operation were displayed and sold. We worked at the Market Street location in partitioned offices and a darkroom constructed in one section of a storage area in the back of the first floor. During the winter months, it was so cold that the chemicals used to develop and fix film and photos froze solid in containers. The *Ashland Daily News* made our engravings. Manual typewriters were used by reporters who wrote stories on sheets of paper that were edited and then sent to a printing plant in the back section of a commercial store on Shamokin Street where the company's first flatbed printing press was located.

Later, the entire operation was moved to a newly constructed building on Sunbury Street, with the editorial offices on one floor and all printing equipment, including linotypes and the flatbed press, in the basement. A section of the basement was partitioned off for a small darkroom.

HARRY JR.: Meanwhile, your personal life was changing. When did you get engaged?

HARRY SR.: I bought the diamond ring for her as a Christmas gift (in 1948) approximately 13 months after I came home from the service, went back to my senior year in high school, and graduated in May as a member of the class of 1948. I still had no steady income except the 52-20 benefit from the G.I. Bill of Rights and the little money I was able to save from odd jobs I picked up after graduation, including sweeping the floor at a furniture store on North Shamokin Street. It was a struggle, but I got the $200 together, bought the ring, and showed it to Beverly's mother before I popped the question to the beautiful young lady who was still a senior in her high school. I think Mrs. Smith was very pleased because Beverly and I were kind of compatible in thinking about our plans for the future. Beverly's dad, who was very quiet at times, didn't say whether he approved or disapproved.

HARRY JR.: Why did you get married so young?

HARRY SR.: What influenced both of us was our close relationship with friends from Tharptown, Mary Bogetti and Charley Wallish, who were married earlier that year during a large wedding that included a big reception dinner at the Union Fire Company social hall. Both of us were in their wedding party, Beverly as one of the five bridesmaids and me as an usher. Mary was slightly younger than Beverly, and Charley was more my age and went to the Army a short time after I enlisted. As usual, Beverly made a pretty picture in her role as a bridesmaid, dressed in a beautiful pink gown that she bought from money she earned working part-time as a clerk at Grant's department store in downtown Shamokin. I was dressed in a blue suit.

HARRY JR.: You got married several weeks after she graduated. Tell me about your wedding. Who attended? Where did you honeymoon? Why was your brother Clyde your best man?

HARRY SR.: Beverly was very happy with our wedding because it wasn't one of those big events that cost a lot of money. In keeping with tradition, Beverly's mother and dad planned it all, and it was beautiful, from the ceremony in the Sunday school room at Trinity Lutheran Church on Sunbury Street, by the pastor, Dr. Harold C. Fry, to a reception at the home of her parents at 23 South Eighth Street in Shamokin. It was a very conservative wedding and reception, but Beverly was very happy because her lifetime dream of getting married in a white gown was realized.

There was no question that Beverly, in her white gown, was the most beautiful bride. And the fact that we got married in the Sunday school room, because the nave was being remodeled and repainted at the time, didn't bother her one bit. She was indeed a very happy bride. A number of the Smiths' relatives from throughout the state, including many from Liverpool, came to the wedding and reception, as did members of my family and several of the buddies I served with during my tour of duty overseas in the United States Army.

Several months before the wedding, I was lucky to have landed a position as a photographer for the *Shamokin Citizen*, and they were represented at the wedding, including George Shroyer and his wife, Shirley, and members of the editorial staff. Many people were there from Happy Hollow, a summer vacation community along Trevorton Road, where Beverly's parents owned a cottage.

Beverly selected her sister-in-law, Jean Smith, as her maid of honor. Beverly thought, and I agreed, it would be appropriate for one of my family serve as my best man. So I selected Clyde to represent my family for that honor and my friend Charley Wallish to be the usher. It was a very brief ceremony, after which we went for a ride through Tharptown and then had pictures taken at Keith Haupt's Studio on Market Street. Our reception was held at Beverly's parents' home on Eighth Street with delicious food and a wedding cake.

After the reception, Beverly and I went on an abbreviated honeymoon, a weekend trip to Harrisburg and Hershey Park. I didn't own a car, so her dad graciously offered us his 1940s Chevrolet so Beverly and I could go on the weekend honeymoon. When we returned on Sunday night, we began a one-year residence at her parents' house on South Eighth Street, where Beverly grew up.

Harry Joseph Deitz and Beverly Jane Smith on their wedding day, June 25, 1949.
They were married in the Sunday school room at Trinity Lutheran Church because
the sanctuary was being renovated at the time.

HARRY JR.: Tell me about your first apartment.

HARRY SR.: That's a story by itself. We knew that we wanted to go into housekeeping by ourselves and made plans by buying a kitchen set and several appliances, including a ringer-washing machine on a time payment. At the same time, Beverly's dad found a headboard and other parts to a bed set. As a carpenter, he spent many hours sanding and finishing the new bed as a gift to help augment what we purchased on our own. We became friends with several couples, including Jack and Sarah Paretti and Bob and Betty Sherman, who were married one week before our wedding. Betty was a classmate of Beverly, and Jack was a classmate of mine in our sophomore year at Coal Township before he went into the Merchant Marines. Beverly and I were close friends of both couples, and we got together frequently.

Jack and Sarah lived on the third floor of the Turner Apartment building on Market Street, and when a unit on the second floor became available, they told us about it. We looked into renting it for $10 a week. It was a very small apartment containing a tiny kitchen with an ice box and a corner space that we called our living room. A bedroom area was partitioned by a draw curtain between the kitchen and the living space. The window in the living area fronted Market Street.

The apartment itself was small, very inconvenient, and was infected with water bugs. I was ready to move out shortly after we moved in. Beverly never complained. She said it was our first home, and she was proud of it. In fact, she made it very livable, cleaning up every nook and corner, getting rid of the insects, and even sewing curtains for the front windows. Her ability to make something beautiful and appealing was something special during our entire married life together.

While the apartment didn't appeal to me at first, its location was ideal. It was across the street from the *Shamokin Citizen* editorial office, where I sometimes worked day and night. I learned to love the apartment.

HARRY JR.: Tell me about your early married life. Did you have a television? What kind of meals did you have? What did you do for entertainment? Were you finally able to afford to buy things? I sense that even though things were better, you still struggled.

HARRY SR.: It was more than a struggle the first year, but I was thankful to have full-time employment because jobs were hard to find following World War II. The company paid me $20 for a 46-hour work-week, but that was augmented by a stipend from the federal government when I filed for an on-the-job training benefit under the G.I. Bill of Rights. So my net take-home pay after deductions for taxes, FICA, and another charge I don't remember was less than $35 per week. Beverly maintained a tight budget, and we managed to have a few dollars as spending money at the end of the week. Beverly had several part-time jobs, but we later decided that she didn't need to work as long as we balanced our budget each week. I was happy about that.

During that time, our major entertainment was listening to the radio, reading funny books, and going to the movies at 50 cents each a clip. Once each week, most Saturday nights, we would get together with other couples, and the guys would go and buy chicken platters. We'd have a friendly dinner together for a minimal cost of about $2.50 per couple. Television in the Shamokin area didn't come into play because getting over-the-air signals was difficult due to the community being nestled between mountains.

HARRY JR.: When did you get your first car? How did you get around before that?

HARRY SR.: For a long time, we didn't have a car of our own. The company I worked for provided two vehicles for reporters, and I used one for assignments. The cars were kept in a storage garage on Sunbury Street, near Market, and during the daytime, they were parked in a lot adjoining the newspaper's office on Market Street. When the both of us wanted to go someplace, we walked, rode a bus, or depended on several friends who owned used cars.

HARRY JR.: Several times you moved in with mom's parents. Why?

HARRY SR.: We lived with Beverly's mother and dad for some of the early years of our marriage and, from my salary, paid them $10 weekly for room and board. We didn't complain about that.

There were many reasons that was necessary. Once because of a sudden health issue for Beverly and several times when decisions required us to make adjustments while either moving or building our new home in Overlook. Mom and Dad Smith always welcomed us with open arms because they lived in a large home on Eighth and High Streets, and moving in with them for short periods helped fill voids in their lives.

Our mother's parents, Jacob Leroy and Mary Barbara Smith at the side yard of the house on South Eighth Street, where our parents lived several times early in their marriage. Below is a recent picture of the house.

Our first move back to the Smith home was after being located in the Turner Apartments on Market Street. Beverly had a miscarriage and was unable to climb the steps to our apartment on the second floor. She needed attention after she underwent surgery, and having someone with her every day while I was at work was the answer. Grandma Smith said, "Why don't you come up here and keep your apartment open if you want to?" But I wasn't going to keep the apartment because we didn't know how long it would be.

So we moved up with them for a while, and you were born when we lived there in 1952. Then the apartment opened at Martini's. My brother Ben and (his wife) Sis rented the one apartment on the second floor, and we were on the third floor in the back. We were there for quite a while. It was a good place. The only problem we had was the heat on cold nights. There wasn't enough heat. I'd have to call the furnace man every once in a while to fire up the furnace because you were getting sick. You got sick a couple of times with bad chest colds that were almost pneumonia.

We were there a couple of years until around June of 1954. Right before Barbara was born, we moved to Sunbury Street. There was an attorney whose sister owned the house on Sunbury Street, and they had it up for rent. We stayed there till about 1955 or '56, then had to buy the house or move. We liked it there, and I didn't want to move again. I ended up moving anyhow.

In the late '50s, I had an opportunity to go to Milton and work for a daily paper. For a short time during the summer of 1957, I commuted every day. So we rented a house close to the printing plant in Milton, where I worked as a photographer and reporter. The following summer, I was offered a position with the *Shamokin News-Dispatch*. Our house on Sunbury Street in Shamokin that we bought several years previously was occupied under a rental agreement with a schoolteacher and his family, So we had to move in with mom and dad for a short time until the rental contract expired.

Then in the 1960s, there was an opportunity to purchase lots in Overlook, and Beverly's dad and mom helped purchase two for us. The stage was set to build our dream home, but to get started, we needed to sell the home on Sunbury Street for a down payment. We had a buyer, and we quickly closed the deal and then lived again with Mom and Dad

The first house our parents owned—111 West Sunbury Street. At that time, in the late 1950s, it was half of a double and shared a side porch with the house on the other side.

Smith until the summer of 1965, when our new home on Overlook Blvd. was ready. That beautiful brick ranch home and its view of the valley below was the culmination of a dream for the two of us.

HARRY JR.: When and how were you able to buy the house on Sunbury Street? Where did you get a down payment and a mortgage? What attracted you to that house?

HARRY SR.: For several years while I worked for the weekly paper, we had rented the western side of a half double home at 111 West Sunbury Street for $40 a month. While working at the weekly paper, I still earned a minimal salary. The owner and realtor of the house we rented came to us and said they had a buyer but offered the house to us for $5900. The pressure was on us.

We had a little money in a savings account from some photo activity I was doing in my free time for the county coroner and law enforcement groups as well as some individuals, including couples getting married, but there was an insufficient amount in that account to meet the down payment requirement for an extended bank loan. So, my only alternative was to ask the company's president where I worked, to advance me the difference at an interest rate of six percent with payments deducted from my salary over one year. Again, I used the G.I. Bill of Rights to obtain a government-backed bank loan of six percent at the time to close the deal on buying the house. We signed the mortgage for the house with Shamokin Banking and Trust Co. What attracted us to buy the house? Well, it was centrally located in a good neighborhood with friendly neighbors and close to schools and walking distance for church, grocery stores, and other conveniences.

HARRY JR.: You used to get together with other couples during those early years. Who were they, and what did you do for entertainment?

HARRY SR.: The Cultons and Kerns, as well as other couples in our group, were close friends from Tharptown and school. They were in the same boat as Beverly and me in that all of us were struggling to live a life of comfort with a minimum financial income. Jake Kern worked in Williamsport and commuted daily, as did Dukey Culton, who worked in Enola near Harrisburg. Jake's wife, Doris, was a classmate of Beverly's at Shamokin. Duke was a bosom friend of mine since early childhood in Tharptown. None of us could say we were well off financially, but we got together each Saturday for chicken platters and drinks and just a friendly time with as little expense as possible. In the summer, the group held picnics or went on fishing trips to nearby streams and parks. It was our entertainment at a cheap price.

HARRY JR.: What were your feelings when you had your first child?

HARRY SR.: Beverly and I were convinced that when she conceived, it was not only a blessing but a miracle from God. In the early years of our marriage, she had a miscarriage, followed by a problem with an ovarian cyst, requiring surgical removal of the affected ovary. The chances of her getting pregnant were about 50 percent, considering she had only one ovary. So we put all our trust in the hands of God.

Meanwhile, we had several discussions with our pastor, Dr. Harold Fry, about the possibility of adoption. He suggested we wait for several months. Not long after that discussion, God answered our prayers.

Mom and Harry Jr. in 1953, when he was 1 year old.

Beverly conceived, and on the early morning of March 8, 1952, we became the proud parents of a beautiful baby boy, delivered at the maternity suite of what was then known as Shamokin State Hospital by our personal and friendly family physician, Dr. William B. Lewis.

By Beverly's suggestion, the new gift from God was named Harry Jr. The maternal grandparents, Roy and Mary Smith, beamed with happiness as they celebrated the arrival of their third grandchild, two of whom were born to Warren and Jean (Sorenson) Smith earlier at Racine, Wisconsin. Harry Jr. was born while we were residing in Grandpa and Grandma Smith's home on South Eighth Street.

HARRY JR.: Tell me about having your second child, a girl. How did you view your life as your family came together?

HARRY SR.: We discussed the possibility of having a second child early in 1954, and if it were a girl, our family would be complete. Again, the love of God smiled on us that our plans for a beautiful family were complete. Barbara Christine, named after her grandmothers, Mary

Barbara Smith and Christine Augusta Deitz, was born at Shamokin State General Hospital on the morning of October 24, 1954, ushered into the world by Dr. Lionel Gates, the chief surgeon at the medical center.

Barbara never saw her paternal grandfather, whose name also was Harry Deitz. He died five months and 16 days before she was born. She was the only granddaughter on the Smith side. We lived in the western side of a half-double dwelling at 111 West Sunbury Street, having moved to that location only several months before Barbara was born.

HARRY JR.: Eight years later, you would have a surprise bonus child. Were you more shocked or happy?

HARRY SR.: Surprise is right. But it was a welcomed surprise. Terry Leroy made his debut in this world around 3 o'clock on the afternoon of October 3, 1962. I had just returned home from work at the *News-Dispatch* when Beverly told me the time had arrived. During the change of shifts at the Shamokin State General Hospital, two registered nurses assisted a doctor with the delivery. Harry Jr. and Barbara had gone with their grandmother to town from our Sunbury Street home, and when I returned from the hospital, I had to drive around town looking to find them and give them the news they had a new baby brother.

HARRY JR.: You worked for the *Citizen* for about eight years. Describe your job during that time. Did you like what you were doing? Did the job change?[8]

HARRY SR.: I worked under three editors at the *Citizen*—Jerry Gallagher of Hazleton, Ed Brown, who was imported from somewhere in New York, and Chester Moore from Lebanon, a convert from office clerk for a coal company to reporter and then to editor. Some of the other employees were Kenneth Barber and Joseph Karpinski, who was the sports editor. George Shroyer was the publisher, and Betty Edwards was the receptionist. Another reporter, in later years, was Harold Barnhart, who formerly worked for *The Danville News*. And Ray Shaffer, who later went to work at the *News-Dispatch*. John Shroyer had a column they called "They Tell Me." It was all political stuff.

The first year, George Shroyer (John's son) was very unhappy with Gallagher because he was one of those guys who would wait till the last minute to do what had to be done. He'd wait till Monday or Tuesday to

Harry Deitz during his days as a reporter for the *Citizen*.

start putting things together for Thursday's paper. George Shroyer fired him a week before Christmas.

Then they brought a guy in from New York. Ed Brown was his name. He was a very experienced newspaperman. He was on the wagon. He was an alcoholic, and he went off cold turkey. One night, he got so tense that he went across the street to Harry's (bar) and got drunk. He was fired the next day. Beverly and I took him back up to New York. I had a car that I bought. It was a Chevrolet. I took him back up to New York to his house. His mother was very upset, and she said, "Did he get fired for drinking again?" He was a good friend, and he knew the ins and outs of the newspaper business. He was very good.

While my work was strictly on photography, I was interested in becoming a reporter and spent whatever free time I had studying and taking special courses. I still had stuff coming from the G.I. Bill of Rights. Chet Moore had taken a course through the Newspaper Institute of America, and I decided I would take the course in my spare time. The G.I. Bill of Rights paid for it, and it was out of Columbia University in New York. They had guys who were really experienced newspaper guys. They'd send you some straight information about a fictitious incident, and you'd have to write a story about it, and they'd criticize it. By the time I was done with that, my G.I. Bill of Rights entitlement had run out. I had moved from an apartment to a house on Sunbury Street, and I had gotten a G.I. Bill loan at six percent. I thought I better start learning how to write.

By the end of my eight years with the *Citizen*, I had become a full-fledged double-duty reporter and photographer. In that time, I had gained the respect of police officers and other law enforcement authorities, political leaders, and other groups, including fire fighters and hospital staff members, who were my primary contacts when some spot news events occurred.

Time meant nothing when I responded to the police or anyone else for coverage of major news events in all kinds of weather, for which I never received overtime pay. My reward, even when I suffered frost-bitten ears and feet while covering the ABC Row fire in the Fifth Ward one year, was my satisfaction that I was doing what I was hired to do and at the same time I was serving the public.

In the meantime, some of the pictures I took were hitting the big time—The Associated Press and United Press International.

HARRY JR.: How did you build such great contacts early in your career, especially for spot-news events?

HARRY SR.: When I started, I just hit it lucky because the paper had a car that I could use on assignments, and the car was kept at a storage garage down on Sunbury Street. Fortunately, the state police also kept their cars there because their barracks was in the next block. Later on, we lived right across the street from where the police barracks were. I made arrangements with the guy that was the night watchman there that when the police cars would go out, he'd give me a call and tell me where they were going.

Through that, I was able to make good contacts with the police force. When I'd go out on an accident, they would say to me, "Would you mind taking a couple of extra pictures for us that we could use in court?"

I said, "Sure, why not?" I never charged them; I just gave them to them. That took off. There were several cases where there were bad accidents, and the pictures showed who was at fault. And when they'd come up in court, the police would win the case. That's how I got started in criminal photography. My pictures were always used to explain what happened. I'd take skid marks and everything else for them. I made good contacts, first with the state police and then with all the other police too.

We moved into a home on Sunbury Street right across from the barracks. We were sitting on the front porch one night, when about six or seven cops ran out of the barracks carrying shotguns. I hollered across the street, "Hey, what's going on?"

They hollered back, "There's a shooting in Tharptown."

Then things turned. I really established a name. The good thing was, I had the in, and I'd go out on a police case, and I knew what was going on. At the same time, I knew what I should tell the public and what I shouldn't tell the public. And they appreciated that.

I was the only person at the newspaper at the time that was a combination reporter and photographer.

HARRY JR.: Tell me about when you lost your job at the *Citizen* in 1957.[9]

HARRY SR.: What happened was that my name got circulated. I had jobs galore I could have gone to. But I stayed with the weekly paper, and

I was there for about eight years. And then, one spring, somebody asked me to take a picture of a confirmation class at one of the churches. I said "sure." And they wanted to know if they could put it in the paper, and I said "sure." They wanted copies of the pictures, and I thought I might as well make a couple of bucks. I decided to give them a copy of the picture for 50 cents apiece. So I bought my own supplies and did my own darkroom work. I sold 24 pictures. It was $12.

Well, the guy in charge of the paper thought that I should turn that money into the company. I did it on my own time on a Sunday morning, made the pictures up on my own time, and they wanted me to turn the money in. I didn't think that was right. And I used my camera. I said, "Why in the world should I do that?"

It came to the point where he said, "If you don't turn the money in, we're going to separate."

I said, "Well, we're going to separate." So I didn't have a job. I went home. I had two young kids at home, a mortgage on the house. That was a Monday morning.

HARRY JR.: How did you feel when you went home on the day you lost your job at the Citizen? How did mom react? Were you worried, or did you feel you could find something else right away?

HARRY SR.: I was devastated for a brief time until I gathered my thoughts and remembered that only a short time before that incident in 1957 occurred on Monday, following the July 4th weekend, I was offered employment at not one but several daily newspapers in the region. Beverly told me that I shouldn't worry, suggesting that both of us put the problem of my being unemployed in the hands of God. And God responded as word spread quickly.

A meeting was scheduled with Bill Hastings, publisher, and Charlie Johnson, editor of *The Milton Standard*. The following Monday morning, I began an enjoyable association with the Milton newspaper and its executives and four-member editorial staff, who welcomed me. Later that fall, we rented a house one block away from *The Standard*'s building and across Broad Street, where the company's cars were stored in a public garage.[10]

4

A Talented Workaholic

The hardships during our father's early years would forever cast a shadow over his outlook and his approach to life. He never would take anything for granted. He also would become obsessed with avoiding personal failure and not disappointing those who crossed his career path.

As children, one thing we knew about our father was the importance of his work. His job often came first. Despite our resentment for that, we eventually came to understand that he couldn't risk slipping back into the life he had known as a boy. Family drives on Sunday afternoons were often tied to a picture he had to take or a story he was doing. When the fire alarm rang, he was out the door, regardless of the hour. If someone at the newspaper needed him or someone he knew in the community wanted a favor, our family plans were put on hold or canceled. He was a classic old-time newspaperman who was on duty day and night. That's the way it was. In the truest sense, he was—and is—a workaholic.

He never forgot the struggles of his early life, including the meager meals from his childhood. So when he finally had a steady income, he looked forward to regular, hearty food—meat and potatoes—every night. In fact, mashed potatoes. My sister and I grew so tired of mashed potatoes at every meal that we refused to eat them for many years when we became adults. For the rest of his life, our father has loved them.

He also never forgot the lack of necessities during his childhood, so he instilled in his children the importance of not spending frivolously and not wasting. In his mind, the progress he had made in his life was not sufficient. He wanted more for us. In fact, he insisted on it.

When his newspaper salary wasn't enough, he would take pictures of class reunions and sports teams to earn extra money. From his personal experience, he realized the importance of education, so when it came time for me, and then my sister, to go to college, he and I started taking wedding photos to cover the costs. As with many things with our father, it wasn't done halfway. It grew quickly into a side business that filled most of our weekends for quite a few years.

Despite the obstacles he overcame and the success he achieved, I always sensed our father felt he was playing catch-up, trying to get ahead but never quite reaching the goals he set for his life. In my adult mind, he did what he felt he had to do for himself and his family.

During the early part of his career, his work dedication and connections allowed him to recover quickly when he suddenly lost his job at the weekly newspaper where his career began. There would be other setbacks, but each time he moved on and came out ahead.

That started with a move to Milton, where he got his first daily newspaper job as a photographer and reporter. It was the only time he and our mother lived away from Shamokin.

Even after returning to Shamokin to work for the daily newspaper a year later, he continued to face challenges that could have destroyed all that he had accomplished. Almost 20 years later, he again faced what he considered unfair treatment—a demotion that was unwarranted and unwise, in our minds—and he would leave that newspaper to work in Reading, where he commuted for several years. However, his attachment to Shamokin led him to return home to finish his full-time career.

During those 40-some years in the newspaper business, he filled a wall with awards for his work as a photographer and writer. He had more news contacts than anyone who worked with him. He was an excellent photographer, from sheet film to digital. He was a very good writer and editor and had few rivals when it came to reporting.

I believe, without hesitation, he was the best newsman in the history of the Shamokin area. And he was the greatest newspaperman I have ever known.

HARRY JR.: Tell me about your move to Milton. What kind of work did you do at Milton?

HARRY SR.: My argument with George Shroyer was on Monday, right after the Fourth of July, and I was on my way to Milton on Wednesday. Meantime I got another call from *The Danville News* and another paper, maybe Dubois. I didn't want to go too far away because I knew eventually Bob Malick (the publisher at the *Shamokin News-Dispatch*) would entice me to come there. Sometime earlier, they had asked me to come. Bob Malick came to my house one day at lunchtime. I didn't feel I was ready to move into a daily paper. I knew I could handle things with the weekly because I had time, but I wasn't ready for the change to a new schedule.

When I first went to Milton, I was just a photographer. They had a problem with their photographer, and they needed a second photographer. The thing was, it was at the time they came out with a machine they called a Scanagraver. The Scanagraver was a thing that you put the pictures on a drum and a piece of plastic, and it made an engraving by scanning it. I was a real whiz at that. Their salesman, Sam Dean, heard about me arguing with George Shroyer and heard that I left. He didn't hesitate to call *The Milton Standard*. By the time I called, they had said, "We heard about you, and you're available."

I said, "I'm more than available; I'm ready."

Charlie Johnson said, "Why don't you come over this afternoon?"

I went up on Wednesday afternoon, and they said, "Can you come to work on Monday morning?"

I said, "I sure can." I became a reporter there, and then I ended up as sports editor. They really liked me, and I liked them, too, because Charlie Johnson was a good leader. He respected people who could do things.

HARRY JR.: You rented out your house in Shamokin and rented a house in Milton. Was that because you knew you would soon return to Shamokin?

HARRY SR.: I had no choice about renting the house out because I had a $40 a month mortgage, and it was the only way I could pay the mortgage by renting the house out for $40.

Bob Malick, the publisher of the *News-Dispatch* in Shamokin, that was the daily paper, was after me. I was reluctant to go because I didn't feel I was capable of working (as a reporter) for a daily newspaper. I didn't feel I had the experience. And I didn't like the idea of being under the gun, the pressure. But he had watched my stuff at the weekly paper, and then he kept after me and said, "When are you going to come to work for us?"

I didn't want to leave Milton right away because they were good to me. That was early in the spring, and they (Shamokin) had an opening when one of their reporters retired in August. He called me again, and I said, "OK, I'll give it a shot." So I went to work for them, and it was almost $100 a week.

And the good thing was, any picture I took, if anybody wanted to order a picture, all that money was mine. That was the difference between what happened at the *Citizen* and while I was at the *News-Dispatch*.

And then the *Reading Eagle*, I used to do their correspondence. They had a Sunday paper that was pretty widespread in the Anthracite area. They'd call me up and ask me if I'd cover something for them on Saturday. The *News-Dispatch* didn't care what I did (on weekends) as long as I was doing work for them too.

So I came back, and I gave the other paper quite a bit of competition. When I came back to Shamokin, I was still on the number one list for the police and the coroner, and now they were calling me and saying: "Harry, we need your assistance. Come out and take a couple of pictures." That's why I never left them down.

We had the house here, and I had to ask the people who rented it to find another place, and they did. They understood.

HARRY JR.: Were you and mom excited about returning home to be close to family and all the contacts you had made during your first eight years in the newspaper business?

HARRY SR.: The problem was that my mom was by herself. Joe was there, but he was up in years. The only person there at the time was Clyde. Mom needed somebody to take care of her. Beverly's dad and mom were still living, but her dad wasn't in real good health. They had no one. It was a good move.

Our friends were all here, and I had established tremendous contacts with the police, politicians, and hospitals—the hospital especially. The nurses there were good. The superintendent was really good. They allowed me a lot of times to talk to patients, particularly when they brought (injured) miners in. I could talk to them.

One reporter covered a mine accident one time and came back with two paragraphs. Tom Brennan (who became executive editor of *The News-Item* in 1976) said to me, "Harry, why don't you see what you can pick up?" I went down to the hospital, and the three of them were all in this one room. I just walked right in and talked to them about this mine explosion. They were pretty upset with the mine operator that he didn't take precautions. I had a first-person interview with all three of them. I came back and wrote about a column and-a-half. A lot of times, they would do that when something big would happen.

My contacts here were tremendous. One guy was an ambulance driver, and they didn't have radios yet. He'd always call me from home and say, "I got a head-on crash." I'd jump in the car and go.

Another reason was the state police barracks was right across the street from our house. Sometimes I'd be sitting on the porch with mom and you kids, and I'd see them coming out of the barracks with a rifle. Their cars were always parked in that garage (in the next block). Joe Sock worked the night shift there at the garage, and he would call me when cops would come in for the cars.

Those were the kinds of contacts I had. It was important to build up those contacts in the years when I worked at the *Citizen*. When something big happened, somebody was calling me. Somebody was saying, "Get ahold of Harry right away."

I'd go out and do work for the police and do all that printing and everything else and never charged them a penny. When a new trooper would come with a family, I'd do a big picture of them, and mom would paint (colorize) it. She'd paint it with heavy oil, and I'd put it in a frame and give it to them, like a welcoming present. You had to do those little things. They always appreciated what I did.

HARRY JR.: You eventually moved from reporting to editing. Tell me about that.

HARRY SR.: In 1968, the paper merged with the *Mount Carmel Item*. They took me off the police beat and put me in as sports editor a year or

Images of our father during his career at the *Shamokin News-Dispatch*. Top, at the center-right desk in the newsroom; above left, reporting and photographing a news event; above right, covering a sports event; far right, above, the *News-Dispatch* building in the 1960s; far right, working at his desk around 1960, and with his 35 mm camera later in his career.

two before that. Then they finally put Jim George in as sports editor and made me associate editor.

In 1976, Paul McElwee (city editor), Bill Dyer (executive editor), and Chet Moore were all the same age. Before they retired, Jack Reid (whose parents owned the newspaper and who had become publisher when Malick retired at the end of 1961) asked them to put a special edition together for the bicentennial. Before that, Tom Brennan was made the executive editor, and I was made the city editor.

HARRY SR.: What was the best picture you ever took?

HARRY JR.: About two months after the first edition of the *Citizen* went to press, we were in an office over on Market Street, and I heard the screeching of this car. I grabbed the camera and ran out, and here this little boy was hit by a car, and they were waiting for the ambulance. In the meantime, the father was inside taking a shower, and he put on his trousers and ran out and picked up the little boy. By that time, the ambulance was there, and he was carrying the little boy to it. The picture tells the story. The little boy lived through it. He was knocked out. Kimber Shaffer was the boy's name. His dad worked in the mines, and he came home just before it happened. A crowd gathered. They all looked like they had tragedy on their faces. It was a picture to me that told the story.

The other picture was St. Edward's church fire. I did the story and pictures on that. That picture went all over the world with The Associated Press. I was a stringer for The Associated Press under Doug Bailey. I won an award for that with the AP. At the time, not many papers were using natural light, and that was a natural light shot.

HARRY JR.: What was the best story you ever wrote?

HARRY SR.: I still think it was a story of two women who had heart conditions and underwent open-heart surgery to replace valves. I'll never forget, my lead to that was: "Their hearts beat without pain. Like any other young people, they enjoy life. They walk normally. They talk as if there is nothing different about them. They laugh. But they seldom cry."

Do you know how that came about? I was the editor in charge of the Saturday paper, and it was still afternoon, and these two girls came in. I asked somebody else on the staff to do it, and they were tied up

'Ball in Cage' Device

Artificial Heart Valves Keep Two Women Alive

By HARRY J. DEITZ

Their hearts beat without pain. Like any other young people they enjoy life. They walk normally. They talk as if there is nothing different about them. They laugh. But they seldom cry.

Limitations in their everyday life are few. They must take time in walking up steps. They are told to avoid any type of emotional excitement. They cannot run or take part in any real strenuous exercise. And they are restricted from doing the family laundry or moving furniture.

Two Shamokin young women are living proof that any person with a congenital heart defect can have a bright outlook on life today because of modern surgical techniques known as a "ball - in - cage" replacement valve.

"Before I underwent surgery, I was told that my life expectancy was very short," said Mrs. Grant T. Wetzel, a 25-year-old housewife of 50 South First Street. "Now I can expect to live as long as any other person in good health."

The same faith in the operation to replace a defective heart valve with a man-made device was echoed by Miss Roseann Schrader, 21, of Trevorton Road, a business education student in Harrisburg, who underwent open heart surgery in the same hospital.

"Mary Wetzel gave me the confidence I needed," said Miss Schrader. "I'm glad I listened to her and I would offer the same type of advice to anyone who is debating about an operation of this kind."

Mrs. Wetzel and Miss Schrader both underwent the heart valve replacement surgery in Presbyterian Hospital, Philadelphia. Dr. Robert Trout, noted heart surgeon, performed the two operations. Each of the young women has the same type of man-made valve inside her heart regulating blood flow through the body.

"This is what it looks like," said Mrs. Wetzel showing a picture of a small plastic device which she called the "Starr-Edwards ball-in-cage" valve. The object is small and shaped like a funnel. It has four cross pins over the top and inside of this is a small white plastic ball.

The valve works on the same principle as the water faucet. It allows blood to flow through one way, but the flow cannot backtrack. The small ball is lifted by pressure, or the beat of the heart, then drops back into position to await the next surge of pressure.

Mrs. Wetzel and Miss Schrader said the special type valves in their hearts are designed to last more than 45 years. The only precaution they must take against the possibility of malfunction is to refrain from strenuous work or exercise. They also must take special medication to keep the blood thin. The man-made valve has func-Turn to Page 7—

Roseann Schrader, left, and Mrs. Grant Wetzel . . . outlook on life now bright.

Clipping of what our father considers his best story.

and couldn't do it. So I talked to the girls while I was putting the paper together for that Saturday afternoon edition.

HARRY JR.: What was the biggest news story you ever covered?

HARRY SR.: The discovery of the bodies of three girls up on the mountain. When they found the bodies, I was on that. Bobby Olcese (of the Shamokin police department) called me in the morning. Earlier I told city editor Paul McElwee, "I'm sitting on one of the biggest stories in this town's history." He wanted me to tell him what it was, and I wouldn't do it. I said: "I can't tell you. I'm sworn to secrecy and confidentiality. When it breaks, you're going to remember that I told you I'm sitting on the biggest story in Shamokin's history."

He said, "You're going to let me know?"

I said, "As soon as it breaks, you'll be the first to know it."

I'm getting ready to go to work on a Monday morning, and I get the telephone call from Olcese. All he said was, "Harry, this is it. Go up to Burnside, and you'll come to a road that goes to the left, and I'll meet you at the entrance. We're sealing off the entrance now." I knew what it was about because I was sitting on it.

On the way up, I stopped, and I called Paul, and I said, "Paul, this is it."

He didn't ask me any more questions. He just said, "OK. You're going to keep in touch?"

I said, "I will." I went up to Burnside, and the cop left me through the line and said, "They're waiting for you." So I went back, and here they found the skeletons of those three girls.

That was what I thought was great confidence between the cops and me. They really trusted me. I kept my mouth shut. I told nobody. I didn't tell your mom. I just told her there's going to be a big story break here one day, and it's going to be one of the biggest this town ever knew.

I got up there and started taking pictures. They were waiting for the medical examiner from Philadelphia to come into the Shamokin airport.

Tom Brennan was fit to be tied because he was on the wire desk at the time. Paul McElwee went out for dinner, and I thought I better call. We didn't have cell phones at the time, so I drove back to Burnside to a private home and called the newspaper. It was after 1 o'clock, and the deadline was 2. I got Tom Brennan and I said: "I have to give you this. You better put something together right away." I dictated to him over the telephone. He was fit to be tied that Paul McElwee didn't tell him in the morning that I was out on something and there was going to be a break. Paul kept his mouth shut, and I respected him for that too.

I dictated the story verbatim to Brennan. I rattled it off about an army of law enforcement officers gathered at this abandoned stripping pit in Burnside, where the skeletal remains of three girls were found in a shallow grave.

I said, "Tom, in the upper left-hand drawer of my desk, there are three pictures of the three girls." So they came out with a Page 1 main story, and we scooped everybody.

The story: On Sunday, October 6, 1974, the skeletal remains of three teenage girls, who were missing since July 19, 1973, were discovered in a shallow grave in the coal strippings south of Shamokin. The girls and three young men had been cruising in the downtown before going to the mountain, where there was an argument, and the men killed the girls. The three males were charged and sentenced to life in prison.

Walnut Towers fire was a big one, too, for me. I did the editing and had a sidebar about two people jumping out of the window onto the roof of the adjoining building. I was the city editor, and it happened in the early morning on New Year's Day, 1977. I covered a lot of it.

The following Friday night, we were all working, and I got the call from Bobby Olcese, and he said: "Harry, Jerry Waugh (the police chief) told me to call you. They're cracking the case about the Walnut Towers fire. There's two guys that are involved, and they're both firemen."

I called Jerry and said, "I don't have anybody to send."

He said: "I want you. Nobody else. You. If you don't come up, you're not getting the story."

I had to go. I wrote that story. It was 11 o'clock. I wrote the whole story that night.

The story: Nine people died in an early morning fire on New Year's Day in 1977 at the Coal Hole bar of the Walnut Towers Motor Inn in Shamokin. A week later, two young firemen were charged with setting the fire at the bar, where they had been drinking earlier on New Year's Eve.

When (tropical storm) Agnes hit in June of 1972, I was the associate editor, and I worked 72 hours around the clock and got soaked.

One of the funniest stories I wrote was of the cops trying to capture this pet monkey. And they were chasing him around a car.

Another funny one was, there was a paint truck from the Department of Highways. My mother went down to the store on the main street in Tharptown, and she was on her way back home, and the paint truck came by, and the hose broke. She got splattered with paint, and the cars parked all along there were splattered with paint. I sent the story and picture out to the AP, and they gave it good play about this 60- or 70-year-old lady getting splattered with paint from the highway paint truck.

HARRY JR.: What story had the biggest impact on you—one you can't forget?

HARRY SR.: A tragedy involving a father who murdered his wife and a young daughter. A second daughter survived the attack and was hospitalized. When I saw her in the hospital, my heart sank because she was a beautiful child and needed prayers for recovery. I remember buying

These are two of what our father considers his best pictures during his newspaper career. Above, a father carries his injured son to an ambulance after the boy was hit by a car. It was several months after our father began his first job in 1949. The boy survived. At right, the fire that destroyed St. Edward's church on Shamokin Street in 1971.

Four of the thousands of photos from our father's long newspaper career.

Above: Miners leave the Glen Burn mine at the end of a shift.

Left: Family members react after a boy died when he was hit by a car while riding his bicycle.

Top right: One of our father's favorites among his pictures.

Bottom Right: A picture our father took in the 1950s of the snowcovered culm bank next to Tharptown.

a teddy bear and taking it to the hospital for her. And I remember writing a sidebar to the top story telling how I felt.

HARRY JR.: When we returned to Shamokin from Milton in 1958, the family became very involved at Trinity Lutheran Church, about two blocks east of our house on Sunbury Street. What did you do at the church?

HARRY SR.: Beverly and I were active members of Christ Lutheran Church when we lived in Milton. So when we returned to Shamokin in 1958, we just continued working with Dr. Harold Fry until he left to accept the pastorate of a church in New York State. But, even as new ministers took over the helm at Trinity in Shamokin, Beverly and I continued to be active as members.

I served on the Boy Scout committee and church council, was Sunday school superintendent, and sang in the church's adult choir. Beverly was very active as a Sunday school teacher and with the ladies group of the church and contributed time and talent in many other ways. When the church administration needed help in any way, both financially and in manpower, both of us were always available.

Our association at Trinity came to an end when the controversy between the pastor at that time and the church council affected our three young children, so we left and became active members of Grace Lutheran Church across town, Beverly serving on the Altar Guild and with the ladies group called Mary and Martha. I served on church council many years, serving as president for one term, and continuing with the choir. Both of us continued attendance at Sunday school classes regularly.

HARRY JR.: You also became a referee for high school football and basketball. Why did you do that? What was your most memorable game? What was your most controversial call?

HARRY SR.: Passing the PIAA examinations for registration in high school football and basketball officiating was a highlight of my life, beginning in 1954 when I was a substitute sports editor for the *Shamokin Citizen*. I became interested while covering sports events at local high schools. Bernie Romanoski, Joe Diminick, and I took the tests together, and we all passed with flying colors. Over the 35 years, I worked many football games at high schools in most sections of central and eastern Pennsylvania and had 20 years of active participation as a registered PIAA basketball official, including many crucial games involving championships.

One experience in football I'll never forget involved Trevorton High School, a powerhouse in the 1960s in what was then the Twin Valley conference. On the first Saturday in November 1962, I joined Ed Piestrak of Williamsport, Al Masciantonio from Mount Carmel, and George "Norge" Dorko from Shamokin in officiating a game between Trevorton and Williamstown at the foundry field in Trevorton. At the start of the game, heavy, dark clouds and a dip in cold temperatures brought the first hint of an approaching snowstorm. By halftime, four inches covered the football field. Snow continued throughout the entire game, and by the end of the third quarter, we were sloshing through about six inches. Trevorton was leading by a 26-0 score, so the fourth quarter was cut to eight minutes, and at the game's end, there were about eight inches on the ground. The team buses were unable to get up to the high school until PennDOT snowplows cleared the highway. Wlliamstown's team stayed overnight in the gymnasium.

The most controversial call I made was in the Eastern Conference Class B game between Bloomsburg and Lakeland at Berwick. Lakeland was leading 20-13, and Bloom was on the 5-yard line with fourth down and goal to go, when the quarterback threw a pass to a wide-open end standing in the end zone. I was the umpire and was under the goal post when I looked to my right. The center on Bloomsburg's team was illegally downfield. The touchdown was negated, and Lakeland ran out the clock to win the game.

HARRY JR.: Your other non-newspaper activity was taking photos of weddings and class reunions. How did you get started with your wedding business? What did that extra work mean for you and your family?

HARRY SR.: I made enough money as a salaried employee at the newspaper to get along, but like all young married couples, we needed a little more to get the extras, going out for a chicken dinner on a specific night, buying needed appliances and paying mortgages and car loans. So when I was asked by a friend to take pictures of his wedding, I accepted the challenge, which led to a spread of word among other engaged

Our father as a football official, top left and below.

couples about a photographer who didn't overcharge but still provided a professional service. My wife joined me by helping set up special poses and ensuring everything was picture-perfect, such as gown flares and other details.

At the same time, I was contracted by representatives of various classes planning anniversary reunions. It was a busy Saturday night some weeks, but we did make a little money for a rainy day. The extra income was used to pay for the college education costs for two of our three children.

HARRY JR.: In 1965, you started construction on your house in Overlook, several miles north of Shamokin. What led you to do that? Tell me how important that was to you.

HARRY SR.: Our plans to build a home in the suburban section of Overlook materialized due to a frightening experience involving our youngest child, Terry, who one night stopped breathing while being rocked to sleep by his mother. The presence of mind by Beverly saved the little guy's life. She reacted immediately, turning him over and slapping his back until his breathing returned to normal.

When we took him to the hospital, there was evidence he had a pulmonary problem, which may have been compounded by dust from the street and possibly emission fumes from vehicles less than 20 feet from the front of our residence on Sunbury Street, where traffic was usually heavy. We decided to move into a clean-air environment in the suburban sector, so we looked over land availability and found one tract in Overlook.

Beverly's dad was happy about our decision and helped our cause by forwarding the amount we needed to purchase two lots. Several friends from church had already built homes in the same development, so it was an ideal location with many people we knew. In the meantime, I had talked to John Reid, publisher of the newspaper where I worked, and received his assurance that my position there was practically secured for me to continue arrangements for selling our home on Sunbury Street and signing the mortgage for a bank loan to proceed when the land was obtained.

Beverly and her dad sat in the office of lawyer Bob Moser, legal representative for the landowner, for the better part of a long day waiting

The house our parents built in 1965 in Overlook.

for him to come back from a court session so the deed to the property he had charge of could be signed. We contracted for the construction of Beverly's dream home with Stan Reed of Trevorton in March 1965, and on the weekend of July 4, we moved into the one-story brick, ranch-type home with a beautiful view from the dining room window of the Weigh Scales valley below.

HARRY JR.: The low point of your career was when you were removed as city editor of *The News-Item* by the publisher, Jack Reid. Tell me about that.

HARRY SR.: He (Jack Reid) did it in a very tactless way, instead of sitting down and talking to me and saying, "Harry, we think you're more valuable to us than being one of the editors."

I came to work, and at the end of the day, Tom Brennan (executive editor) called me into the office and said, "Harry, we're going to change your desk." He didn't tell me I was demoted. Later, I found out from Phil Yucha (general manager and later publisher), who really respected me for the contributions I made to that paper.

Tom Brennan said: "We're going to make some changes. We want you to sit at that desk, and Joe McGlinn is going to sit at your desk." That was a real putdown to me. Two or three years before that, there was a murder in Danville, and Joe McGlinn was the editor there and had a story on this murder with very few details. I knew the guy from the Department of Public Assistance, and this woman who was murdered was some big shot in the Department of Welfare. I wrote rings around Joe McGlinn's story. I had the details about somebody putting a plastic bag over her head and tying it around her neck. She was in the office doing work at night. I had everything, down to the clothes she was wearing.

I thought that was really putting me down. That's the way I felt. Then he (Joe) came to me and said: "Harry, I didn't ask for the job, they gave it to me. They called me in and said, you're going to be the city editor."

I said, "Thanks."

The problem was, it was not done above board. The problem was that they did not call me in, with Tom and him, and tell me what they were going to do and why. I think a lot of it was they didn't want (another reporter) out on the police beat because he didn't have the contacts I had. They wanted me to pick up the slack. They weren't satisfied with what they were getting out of some of the other reporters. They were missing things.

HARRY JR.: How did you respond to what happened?

HARRY SR.: He (Jack Reid) thought I was the best, but he didn't want me to be in the top echelon. There was some undercurrent stuff going on. Some people didn't like me because I was tough on them.

Pattie Mihalik was one of my big supporters on the staff. So was Mary Bartol Santor. Mary came over and talked to me, and she said: "Harry, they're out to get you. They're out to get you out of the job as city editor." She said, "If I were you, I would do my very best job in the new assignment and show them it didn't affect me."

But it did affect me, to no end. I couldn't accept that of all the work I did, going out at all hours of the night and covering accidents and fires when nobody else would do it . . . The Walnut Towers fire was a good example.

I was devastated. I was. I thought the least they could have done was keep me in the position and yet put me out on assignments. I was very disappointed. Not because they did it, but they did it in such a way that it came out of the blue.

I went home and thought about it. I went back up, and Jack Reid and Tom Brennan were down in the basement in the cafeteria, and I went down, and I said I want to know why. Jack Reid didn't tell me I was better off doing reporting work than working with the staff.

HARRY JR.: How were you able to continue working under those circumstances?

HARRY SR.: That was rough. When Jack Reid demoted me, I went off on a tangent. I stopped into Shipe's (bar) every night after work, after a meeting. I would have been an alcoholic. I didn't care anymore. I just reached the point where I said, "What was the use?" I said to myself, "I put my life into helping other people, and I didn't get anything for it but a kick in the teeth from one I thought was one of my best friends." And I had a tough time. I spent more money on beer and good times in a couple of barrooms, and mom stayed at home alone, and yet, she stuck by me. I couldn't ask for anything better. I found all kinds of excuses to go out with the boys. If it wouldn't have been that I got sick—I think I had a touch of hepatitis from drinking so much alcohol—and if I hadn't put my life in God's hands, it wouldn't have worked either. I would have been gone long ago.

That's what makes me mad, or sad because I never told your mom how much she really meant. I wish I did, but I can't now. That's what makes me feel bad at times. Up to the end, she was always supporting me in everything, helping me. God bless her.

HARRY JR.: You didn't leave *The News-Item* right away, but you wanted to get out of there, and so did I. You contacted Al Nerino, who was the number two guy at the *Reading Eagle* at that time and would eventually become the managing editor. Within a year, both of us were working at *Reading*.

I started looking around for another job. Bloomsburg talked to me, and Sunbury talked to me. There weren't any openings. The managing editor at Bloomsburg said I was overqualified, which meant they would have to pay me more than the average reporter. I was willing to go back to being a reporter. So I took Mary Santor's advice, and I swallowed my pride, and I did what I had to do. And they were giving me some stinky assignments. They were trying to put me down.

I called Al that fall when I was demoted. I became resigned to the fact they can put me down if they want to, but they're not going to put me out. I'm going to do what I have to do. All the people came to my assistance. All the cops. All the firefighters, ambulance people, and EMTs. They all backed me up.

They were giving me some stinky assignments to which I couldn't say no. And I did my best. I didn't pull back.

The both of us went down to Reading together (to apply in 1978). I got the call from Al and went down the first week in June 1979. Tom Boland (managing editor) was glad I came. He was good. I didn't stop. I did story after story.

Tom Boland was very impressed with me when I was a reporter there, and he promoted me to assistant city editor on January 3 over some old-timers, who were very upset by Boland's selection. I couldn't blame them because I was there only six months. I retained the position until early in 1982 when the *Reading Times* and the *Eagle* staffs merged. There were changes in the editorial positions, and I was renamed copy editor. That was another kick in the teeth, but again I proved myself when in the early months of 1982, I was assigned by Nerino to supervise the production of the *Eagle*'s first business review section. It turned out to be very profitable and successful editorially. The response by readers and advertisers was very positive.

HARRY JR.: *I had moved from a weekly paper in 1975 to become the sports editor at* The News-Item. *In 1978 when my father's job was changed, I took it personally too. It was mainly the unfair treatment of my father, but I also lost confidence in my future there. We both went to* Reading *to apply soon after the demotion. I wanted to work in sports, and there was an opening in that department at* Reading *before the end of the year. I started there in December, and my father joined me there the following summer as a reporter and then assistant city editor. I remained at the* Eagle *for 39 years and became editor-in-chief in 2008. I retired in 2018.*

How did you get to know Al Nerino at the *Reading Eagle*?

HARRY SR.: There was a city editor at the *Eagle* who came to Shamokin several times to attend events of the Traveler's Protective Association, including speaking at annual banquets as a high-ranking rep of the state and national TPA offices. Your mom and I attended most of those events, and the *Eagle*'s city editor was impressed by my coverage and the fact that I took photos too. He always asked me when I was "coming to Reading to work for the *Eagle.*"

At the same time, my name was given to Ken Newbould (Sunday editor) through Ted Jones, with whom I was acquainted when he was a reporter at *The Danville News*. Ken asked me if I would do some stories for the Sunday *Eagle*, and then John Smith also asked me to cover high school sports on Saturdays, especially during the tournaments.

Al Nerino was involved with the production of the Sunday edition then, and I got many calls from him to provide features and cover spot news events when they occurred on a Saturday, including parades throughout the Anthracite region. There were many phone calls between us, and there were times I would make a trip to Reading on Saturdays to hand-deliver film. Nerino was there many times, and we often discussed our experiences in officiating high school football games.

In fact, one of my jobs during my early years at the *News-Dispatch* was to serve as public relations coordinator for the newly organized Anthracite Catholic League, and one of my duties was to assign officials for all the league games. Al Nerino was on the list of approved officials, and I assigned him to many league games each year.

HARRY JR.: Considering your bad experience at *The News-Item* several years earlier, why did you leave Reading in 1982 and return to Shamokin to finish your career?

HARRY SR.: It was a necessity. Your grandmother Smith was having several health issues, including congestive heart failure, requiring periodic hospitalization, and Beverly and I had assumed caregiver roles for my mother and then her (Beverly's) cousin, Margaret Sargeant, both of whom were experiencing several health issues.

Meanwhile, *The News-Item* was missing many spot news stories and pictures, and with the advent of digital technology, I was asked to return to *The News-Item* with the title of regional editor at the same salary I was getting at Reading. Reid and Brennan also agreed to my retention of seniority and continuation of my years of service, which meant I was entitled to all benefits of an employee with 20 or more years of service. The mortgage on our house was paid, and buying a home in Reading or even renting an apartment would have created a financial hardship at my age.

HARRY JR.: Were things different when you returned to Shamokin?

HARRY SR.: They respected me when I returned. Yes, they did. I came back in November of '82. I saw Phil Yucha, the general manager, and he was so glad I was coming back. He said: "You don't know how bad they missed you. When you were here, we didn't have to worry about anything." I picked up where I left off. The cops welcomed me back. The firefighters welcomed me back. Everybody seemed to be very happy about it.

When Thompson (Corporation) bought the newspaper, Jack Reid had to pull up stakes, so Phil was named the publisher. He did a lot for me. Phil was one of the greatest.

HARRY JR.: Looking back, what do you consider your greatest skill or talent, and who inspired it?

HARRY SR.: My greatest gift was taking pictures; There's no doubt about that. I came home from the service, and I had a little 35mm camera, and I didn't get the 4x5 Crown Graphic until I accepted the job at the *Citizen*. I think John U. Shroyer was an inspiration, because when I went to talk to them, John U. Shroyer said, "Can you take a picture and make it nice, and that these people will like it, and put it in the paper?" I said: "I would like to think I could. I have all the technical skills."

When I think back, Bob Malick wanted to hire me when I worked at the *Citizen* about two or three years before I had my problem with George, and he was impressed that I would get up at all hours of the night and in all kinds of weather and go out and take pictures.

HARRY JR.: You started your career using a manual typewriter and now use a laptop computer. Which was easier for you and which would you prefer?

HARRY SR.: As long as I can understand the laptop, I think it's better. But there was something about using a typewriter that inspired you. If you sat down at a typewriter and listened to those keys bouncing back and forth, it built a fire under you. You would sit down and start typing until that doggone typewriter started smoking.

HARRY JR.: Along the same line, you learned photography using a 4x5 camera, sheet film, and a darkroom with an enlarger and chemicals. Now you use a digital 35mm camera, memory cards, and a laptop computer. Do you miss the old days?

HARRY SR.: It was a way of life. I got used to it. I knew how to process it because I did it in the service. It was just a way of life. It was something I had to do. There were professional labs, but when you went out on a news case, you couldn't send it to a professional lab and wait for them to return. You had to do them right away.

When I went out with the 4x5, I had to carry a suitcase practically filled with film or a film pack. You got 12 exposures in this one pack. As you pulled out the tab, it would pull the film behind it. When I take pictures for the coroner, I take up to 100 pictures at a time. Can you imagine me taking even 50 slides out on a case right now? I couldn't handle that.

The same with electronic strobes. They didn't come into play until halfway through my work at the *Citizen*. I used those miniature flash-bulbs. A lot of times, I burned my hand trying to change them.

HARRY JR.: Wasn't there something special about going out and taking a picture and not actually getting to see it until you got into the darkroom and developed the film?

HARRY SR.: You always had apprehension about how the picture was going to come out. You never knew. Don't forget, everything was manual back then. Your focus had to be done manually. Your depth of field. You had to worry about whether the people in the foreground were in focus and the people in the background were in focus too. You had to worry about exposure. And then you had to set all your things by hand.

The problem today is they don't utilize cropping and composure as much as they should. They just go out and line up the people and take the picture. They don't look for something different.

Paul Vathis was a friend of mine, and he worked for AP. He took a picture one time, and you would never think it was a Pulitzer Prize winner. It was a picture of Ike Eisenhower and Jack Kennedy walking up a path, the backs of them just walking up the path, but you could tell who they were. He won a doggone Pulitzer Prize for that.[11]

HARRY JR.: What else changed from early in your career?

HARRY SR.: When I went out on a story, I had to retain a lot of that in my mind. You either wrote the stuff down in a notebook with a pencil, or you had to remember it. I think it was good for your mind. Now they use recording devices for everything. It really changed.

I had a case where there were three miners trapped in a mine up on Bunker Hill. We got the call at 11:45. We're an afternoon paper. Our deadline was 2 o'clock. I ran up on that thing and got all the information I needed and then came back and wrote a full-length-column story for that afternoon paper. That one won a PNPA award for deadline coverage.

HARRY JR.: Who had the biggest influence on your career?

HARRY SR.: There were quite a few. Charlie Johnson, Bob Malick, Phil Yucha, Chet Moore, Paul McElwee, Bill Dyer, Tom Brennan, and Jack Reid influenced my career. Bob Malick, who was my original publisher at the *News-Dispatch*, was one of the best. Bob Malick was a newsman.

I mentioned Jack Reid's name out of respect. He did give me a job. He did send me to different places. Jack Reid's mom and dad (who owned the *News-Dispatch*) liked me. They respected me. I got note after note from Jack Reid's mother about how pleased they were that I worked for them.

HARRY JR.: Why were you a good newsman?

HARRY SR.: I put myself in the position that the other people were in about whom I was writing. I didn't believe in saying nasty things about people. I always believed in being fair with the people I talked to and the news events I covered.

I prided myself in trying to give the whole story and what people wanted to read. As you said in your story, supper would wait. I put my heart into what I was doing. I always wanted to do a good job and didn't want to tramp on people's toes.

You had to be motivated to do things, even when you went out on an ordinary story. You had to find something to motivate you. There were many stories that I did that were dreaded. There was nothing to them, but you had to find something in there that lit a fire under you. That was my reason for success because I'd always find that little something that ignited me.

HARRY JR.: Have you felt appreciated and respected during your career?

HARRY SR.: Some people appreciated me. People like Phil Yucha. He really appreciated what I could do and how I could do it. And Jack Reid had confidence in me, but he never expressed it. He never came to me and patted me on the back and said good story, until after he demoted me, and then he sent me a note (after a big story), and your mom put on it "the first," and she knew that. She knew I never got credit for anything.

Paul McElwee was another one who liked me and depended on me. He would call me and ask me to go out on something, and he knew it would get done.

The thing about it was, when the cops told me something, they knew it was in confidence, and they knew I wouldn't reveal it to anybody. And that earned their respect. A lot of reporters today, they won't do that. They'll break that confidence just for the sake of getting a scoop.

I felt that confidence was more important to me and them than me breaking it and writing a story about it. If there were something they could do that would give me the break on it, they would do it. They knew I would be quiet. Even today, I go out on a case with the coroner and police, I know many things that are going on, but I can't tell anybody. You have an obligation, sure, but you have an obligation too to keep your mouth shut to maintain the contacts you have.

HARRY JR.: You were a classic workaholic. Tell me about your devotion to your work.

HARRY SR.: I never regretted giving time to my job as a reporter, photographer, and editor, even though it took me away from my family for periods, often lasting hours. As a journalist and photographer for daily newspapers, it meant that I was obligated to the public, whose thirst for news events never slowed down. I committed to keeping them informed about what was happening in their neighborhood, in their community, and in the county where they resided. That commitment not only involved reporting on tragedies but coverage of municipal and county government actions and other activities, social and otherwise. Serving as a reporter on a daily newspaper is not only a job but a responsibility of writing an accurate account of whatever activity by the public is covered. Reporting is a responsibility to report in story form all events that satisfy the public's thirst for news.

HARRY JR.: You won a lot of awards for your newspaper work. Which one was the most special to you?

Above: A basement wall covered with some of the many awards our father received during his newspaper career. Below: Holding one of his many state awards.

HARRY SR.: A crowning achievement for any person working in print or electronic media as a professional journalist or photographer is to be singled out as the recipient of prestigious awards. Every time I received recognition of this sort, I felt honored because of the competition in certain categories with many of the top reporters and photographers in the state and the nation.

In my long career, two of what I consider top honors weren't winners of top awards but were recognized for their news value and just being considered part of prominent programs. In other words, I didn't get a trophy or an engraved certificate, but I did have the satisfaction of knowing the special submissions were among the best for consideration. So, the St, Edward's Church fire didn't win the Pulitzer Prize, but its acceptance as a nominee was an honor itself.

Several months after I joined the editorial staff of the *Shamokin News-Dispatch*, I covered a motor vehicle accident near Sunbury that claimed the lives of five teenagers. A sidebar of the main story I wrote about that accident was on activity in the morgue at the hospital in Sunbury, with details that emphasized traffic safety to avoid any similar accidents in the future. Congressman Ivor D. Fenton selected that story for publication on Page 999 of the *Congressional Record* on February 11, 1959. Many thanks to Father Woodrow Jones, pastor of St. Edward's Church, for endorsing the fire photo (1971), and to Robert Malick, publisher of the *Shamokin*

Anger, Sorrow, and Disgust Displayed in Hospital Morgue

EXTENSION OF REMARKS
OF
HON. IVOR D. FENTON
OF PENNSYLVANIA
IN THE HOUSE OF REPRESENTATIVES
Wednesday, February 11, 1959

Mr. FENTON. Mr. Speaker, the terrible loss of life in the ever-increasing highway accidents is causing consternation among our citizens in all sections of the country. The heartaches which result from these accidents are in most instances beyond description.

A very fine article appeared in the January 26 issue of the Shamokin News-Dispatch following a head-on crash which resulted in the death of four persons. This article, written by Staff Writer Harry Deitz, gives a heart-rending account which inspired the headline, "Anger, Sorrow, and Disgust Displayed in Hospital Morgue." I ask unanimous consent to extend my remarks in the RECORD and include this article which might in someway contribute to serious reflection in our efforts to eliminate this unwarrantable loss of human life on the Nation's highways.

ANGER, SORROW, AND DISGUST DISPLAYED IN HOSPITAL MORGUE
(By Harry Deitz)

A veteran police officer turned away in disgust; a young nurse, her white uniform stained with blood, grimaced and a doctor looked stoically at the three bodies lying in the small morgue.

No one had to say what each was thinking—that another accident involving a teenage driver had taken its toll; that a short time before there was life in each of the three young bodies.

The doctor turned to make notes. "It's a darn shame," he mumbled, "that the State can't do something to stop tragedies like this."

In the far corner of the room, a relative looked at the contorted face of a lifeless

Partial clipping of our father's story in the Congressional Record.

News-Dispatch at the time, for his submission of the accident story to Congressman Fenton.

More than 15 other stories and photographs were winners in annual better writing and related photography contests by the Pennsylvania Society of Newspaper Editors, the Pennsylvania Publishers Association as well as The Associated Press. Other photos I took appeared in *The Saturday Evening Post* (February 29, 1952), *Newsweek* (August 21, 1950), and other national and state publications, including *Fire Engineering* (July 1971).

In the one in *The Saturday Evening Post*, the guys in Wilburton didn't have a fire truck. They had a wagon they took to fires, and they pulled it by hand. I had them pulling this hose rig out of the fire company garage. They still were using it then. The one I took that appeared in *Newsweek* was the one where the guys were playing the slot machine outside of the *Shamokin Citizen* office. The one in *Fire Engineering* was on the cover for the article that fire commissioner Claude Kehler did on the fire at St. Ed's.

HARRY JR.: What is so special about Shamokin, and why do you like it so much that you couldn't leave?

HARRY SR.: I had a lot of friends here. I had a lot of people I grew up with that stayed in Shamokin. I had my job here. I was community-oriented. I just liked the friendliness of the people, especially after I came back from the service. Up till then, a lot of people put me down. I always thought I wasn't welcome, probably because of my social status coming from a poor family.

HARRY JR.: How did you feel when I followed you into the newspaper business? You opened the door for my first newspaper job. Were you reluctant to do that? Were you hoping I would choose another profession?

HARRY SR.: To answer that question, I recall being a part of a conversation you had with your mother one night after I came home real late for supper because I was out on a spot news assignment. Your exact words: "Dad's late for supper again. I don't want a job like he has. You don't have any time to yourself." So you set your goal on being a secondary education major in college, but that changed when you went out student teaching and learned that occupation was not always peaches and cream either. So you did exactly what I did and started as a photographer and then went up the ladder. We weren't the only father-and-son team at *The News-Item* or the *Reading Eagle.* There were a number of them at both places at one time or another.

HARRY JR.: *My father is why I got into newspaper work, even though that wasn't my plan. I went to college and got a B.S. in secondary education with a major in English and a certificate in journalism, which was the only thing Bloomsburg State College offered in that field.*

Early in the summer before my senior year, when I was looking forward to student teaching, my father came home from work one day and said the photographer at the newspaper was going to have surgery and would be out of work for the summer. They needed a temporary replacement. Even though it wasn't an ideal situation for either of us, we both knew it was necessary. Before that, I had some photography experience, but not at the level I needed to be a daily newspaper's primary photographer, even for a few months. My father gave me a crash course on news photography and deadline darkroom work.

My work in that summer newspaper job led to a full-time newspaper job after graduation at a weekly newspaper that the Shamokin newspaper had purchased in Schuylkill County. The newspaper profession was a good move because, through my student-teaching experience, I found out classroom teaching wasn't what I wanted to do.

It was ironic that, like my father, I started my newspaper career as a photographer, then moved into sports writing and editing. There was more irony because my first full-time newspaper job was at The Citizen-Standard in Valley View. My father had started at the Citizen in Shamokin and worked next at The Standard in Milton.

5

Not a Typical Retirement

Because our father lived most of his life determined to avoid the poverty he had known as a boy, there was never a time when he could relax. Work was what he knew and a big part of what he has lived for during his entire adult life.

Dad retired from full-time work in 1992 after a 43-year newspaper career and has done freelance work since then. He hasn't stopped working since 1948, more than 73 years. The photography skills that made his career possible have continued to give him purpose during his retirement. It's his only hobby.

The police scanner blares continually in his house and from the portable unit on his belt. He does official photography work for the Northumberland County coroner. He continues to take pictures of fires, accidents, and crime scenes used by the state police, fire companies, and local newspapers. He takes group pictures at class reunions and family gatherings.

He has a red light in his car, and when he approaches a crime, fire, or accident scene, he has direct access. All of the coroner's staff, police, and firefighters know him. And they respect him.

In June of 2000, our father added another important line to his resume when he became a lay minister. Just as with his newspaper career, he saw it as a calling. So, in his 90s, he still ventures out on Sunday mornings, in all types of weather, to spread the Word of God as a supply preacher for the Lutheran Church.

In retirement, our father has found some time relax, but when his phone rings, it has to be answered.

He believes God has been good to him, charting his path out of poverty, picking him up, and showing him a new path every time he slipped. Now he believes he has a responsibility to help others along their faith journey.

So retirement hasn't meant slowing down too much. Now, instead of going into an office after an assignment to finish his work, he sits down at his computer at home and then emails the pictures to the people who need them. In fact, he spends a lot of his time at his computer, where he also does research and then writes sermons. Occasionally the technology is overwhelming and frustrating for him, but we find it amazing how well he handles it at his age.

No one in the family ever believed our father would be happy without working during his retirement years. He thrived on being needed by people in the community, including newspaper readers, public officials, police, and other first responders. He doesn't deny it, and that obsession probably is what has kept him going strong into his 90s.

When some family members have expressed concern for his safety as he has grown older and continues to go out in all kinds of weather and at all hours of the day and night, others among us have reminded them that he lives for those things. Even if we wanted to, we couldn't take those things away from him.

HARRY JR.: Did you look forward to retirement? Why or why not?

HARRY SR.: I think retirement is a goal of most people employed in the newspaper industry, particularly those involved with meeting deadlines every day as well as withstanding the pressures of getting the facts straight and then writing a story relating the facts to the reader. Truthfully, I looked forward to retirement after 43 years as a reporter, photographer, and editor. But when that time came in 1992, I had some regrets because I wasn't sure I could adjust from being overactive as a newspaperman to a life of leisure. So, at the request of Philip Yucha, publisher of *The News-Item* at the time, I decided to become a freelance reporter-photographer but only when the need existed.

HARRY JR.: Tell me about the work you continue to do in your 90s for the Northumberland County coroner, the state police, the fire companies, and local newspapers.

HARRY SR.: My work in criminal and investigative photography dates back to my early years in the newspaper industry. I was experienced in using the Crown Graphic 4x5 camera, and when I photographed specific events for the newspaper, the police would ask me to take additional photos for them and make prints, if needed, when a specific case went to court. I was called many times as a witness for both criminal and civil cases, testifying that the photos entered as evidence were a true representation of the crime scene or whatever incident was under investigation. In connection with some cases, I was asked to provide photos for the coroner's office and the police.

Now, the police have their own forensic unit equipped with modern technical equipment of all kinds, but I still take photos for the coroner when the need arises. Also, my work for many years has included supplying the fire departments with photos for their records of fires and sometimes accident scenes that involve rescue work.

HARRY JR.: How much has the work you still do helped you during your retirement years?

HARRY SR.: It's something for me to do. It keeps my mind occupied. That has helped me tremendously since mom (Beverly) died. If it wouldn't be for that, I'd be going crazy, and you'd have to put me in a nursing home, or you'd have to put me in a psychiatric ward.

If I had to sit here all day long and think about things, I'd go out of my mind. Definitely. It's been a tremendous help. Not only that, the people involved need me, and that makes me feel that I'm still wanted, and it makes me feel that I'm still appreciated. I have to do things to prove to myself I can continue to do things.

HARRY JR.: Tell me about the book you wrote on the history of Knoebels Amusement Park.

HARRY SR.: After I retired, I did some work for *The News-Item*. Phil Yucha was the publisher. The Union National Bank wanted someone to write a history on the bank. I signed up for that. It was the forerunner of the Knoebels book.

Dick Knoebel called me and asked me if I'd meet with them to discuss writing a book on the history of Knoebels. Later, I found out that Phil Yucha had directed him to me. Dick had called Phil and asked if he

Above: Harry Deitz signs copies of the book (at left) that he was commissioned to write on the history of Knoebels Amusement Park for its 75th anniversary in 2001.

knew anybody who could write this book on Knoebels, and Phil said, "I have the guy for you."

Dick called me and said I'd like you to meet with Buddy (Knoebel) and me. I went over and talked to them, and he showed me a couple of books, one from Hersheypark, that were written. He said, "Go home and think about it." This was a year before the 75th anniversary, and they wanted it done for the anniversary.

I thought about it and talked it over with Beverly, and I said, "I don't think I can do it."

She said, "Why don't you give it a try, and if you can't do it, they'll have to get somebody to finish it."

I went over and met with Buddy and Dick and Joe Muscato, the public relations director. They wanted to know my recompense, and I told them I'd charge them $15 an hour plus expenses. They said it was up to me what I wanted, and if I wanted to wait, they would give me a royalty, or I could have a salary. I didn't know if this was going to sell. How many people are going to come to Knoebels and want to buy a book about their history? That was a mistake because I didn't realize how that would take off.

We signed a contract, and they said, "When are you going to start?" I said, "Tomorrow." This was back in 1999.

They said they wanted it done by the first of 2001. I started working on it in the fall of 1999.

Joe had the presence of mind, when they did articles in the paper on Knoebels, he clipped them and saved them. The big thing they saved, they had a transcript of a tape from Pete Knoebel, right before he died, that traced the history back to the beginning. I got the names of different people who worked there earlier. Fritz Reed was very helpful. He was a historian. I talked to people who worked there and were involved with different things. It all came together.

It came out, and the first printing was somewhere between 2,000 and 3,000. It went like hotcakes. They had a book-signing ceremony two or three weeks before the anniversary. There was a long line of people. I was so tired. I must have signed that day about 500 books. Dick Knoebel, Buddy, Joe, and I were signing the books.

I was invited as a special guest to the celebration in July of the 75th anniversary. It was a big occasion. We didn't have anything in the book about the celebration because they wanted the book done for the celebration. So they got the idea to print a supplement. After the first printing, they put the celebration in the new printing. Now they're in their third printing.

They were selling them for $29.50. And they're still selling them. On eBay, just for the heck of it, I looked it up, and there was a Knoebel's book for sale for $85, a first-edition printing.

HARRY JR.: Workwise, what do you think the next few years will hold for you?

HARRY SR.: As long as my health holds up, I'll work. As soon as I see I can't do it anymore, then I'll have to call it quits. As long as I'm able to walk and think straight and comprehend what I have to do, I'll continue it as long as they want me. As long as the people involved think I'm capable of doing it. I have to do things to prove to myself that I'm able to continue to do it. When I reach that point in life when I won't be able to, I'm just going to hang it up. And then it's going to be a matter of me either going into a nursing home or having a caregiver come in full time. It's going to be one or the other. But hey, 93, if I live four or five more years, I'm going to be fortunate. I don't think I'm going to be able to continue for five years doing what I'm doing and living alone.

HARRY JR.: I know you used to play golf, but I'm not aware of any hobbies you have carried into retirement. Is photography your hobby as well as your profession?

HARRY SR.: That's right. I didn't have anything. My (non-work) time was always spent doing church activities or projects at the house. The problem was that your grandfather never left me do things (house projects). I don't know whether he didn't trust me or he didn't want to reveal any secrets. You know, he was like that. He didn't want to give any secrets out about what he knew. If I wanted to do a project, I had to do it on the sly that he didn't know about it. If he knew about it, he was here with his doggone toolbox. He always took over, and I couldn't do a thing. I couldn't even saw any wood or anything. If he did anything, I was the cleanup guy. I did the cleaning up afterward. That's true. I wanted to do things on my own because I thought I'd learn how to do it. He never let me. He just didn't have any confidence in me at all, or he just didn't want to give me his secrets.

HARRY JR.: Other than newspapers, what career do you wish you had pursued?

HARRY SR.: When I was in my junior year at high school, I thought about the possibility of being an airline pilot or a law enforcement officer, perhaps with the Pennsylvania State Police. But that all changed when I couldn't meet the special requirements for grades in math and several other subjects to seek a career as a pilot and the minimum weight requirement of 170 pounds for entrance into the police academy. Hey,

I weighed 130 pounds soaking wet when I enlisted in the military and didn't weigh much more than that when I was discharged almost one and a half years later. Another problem was that you had to be trained for six months as a cadet at the police academy, which meant being away from Beverly for that length of time.

My outlook for a career changed when I entered the army, and learned to use a professional camera and write inscriptions for the photos I took. When I landed my first job in the newspaper business, I wasn't satisfied with just being a photographer, so I set a goal of being a writer also by studying in special courses offered by the Newspaper Institute of America and credit courses at night in English and economics at Bloomsburg State College.

HARRY JR.: Tell me about your faith. Were you baptized as a child? Were you confirmed? Were your parents religious? Who had the greatest influence on your faith journey?

HARRY SR.: I was baptized in Salem Reformed Church on Pine Street in Coal Township in June 1928 by the Rev. Alvin Dietz, pastor of the church at that time. I don't recall the date of confirmation, but it was quite a number of years later after we had moved to Tharptown. I remember attending Sunday school in the Emmanuel United Brethren Church as a youngster, and the teacher was a Miss Killinger. I think the superintendent at the time was George Frederick.

Both my mother and dad at one time were active religiously, mom as a member of St. Edward's in Shamokin, and I learned from information my daughter got on the family history, dad was confirmed in a church in the Llewellyn area where he grew up. Dad was not very active in any church after we moved to Tharptown. But he still had faith because before he died, he requested to someone in the family that at his funeral, he wanted a special hymn, "Softly, Tenderly, Jesus Is Calling."

My born-again experience came after I met Beverly and after I came home from the service. We went to church meetings, including Luther League, and participated in other activities that involved young people at Trinity Lutheran Church. Many people had an influence on me on my faith journey, so many, in fact, that I can't remember all their names. But, first among them, of course, was Beverly, a beautiful lady with whom I

In 2000, our father became a lay worship leader for the Lutheran Church in America. While facing a medical issue, he was inspired by a sermon based on Luke 6:46:"Why do you call me, 'Lord, Lord,' and do not do what I say?"

was married 70 years and 11 months. She was the greatest influence in what I consider my faith healing.

HARRY JR.: When and why did you decide to become a lay minister?

HARRY SR.: Several years before I retired, I had a health issue that I thought was terminal. So after several months of medication and medical testing, the problem persisted. I was convinced my time on this Earth was slowly coming to an end. But Beverly and two former neighbors, Ralph and Jane Neely, convinced me not to give up but put the issue in the hands of God. This advice came several days before I entered the hospital as a patient for another battery of tests to find the problem. It was a Sunday morning when I was watching Dr. James Kennedy's televised worship service from Fort Lauderdale, Florida, and I heard him preach the sermon titled: "Why call me, 'Lord, Lord,' and do not do what I say!" I felt like he was talking directly to me. When the program ended, I prayed that if God found the answer to my health problem, I would dedicate the rest of my life to His service.

Well, God answered that prayer, and when the results of the new tests came back, the problem was solved, and I was on the way to a complete recovery from a hidden kidney stone. So, I kept my promise to God and began a new career in life by being a circuit speaker in area churches.

A short time later, the Upper Susquehanna Synod, Lutheran Church in America, offered a program for a two-year study in theology to become an Authorized Lay Worship Leader. I was accepted with 22 other candidates from central Pennsylvania. We completed the required study and were inducted during a formal ceremony in 2000 at the synod assembly at Susquehanna University, Selinsgrove.

HARRY JR.: *For more than 20 years, our father has preached at churches within a 25-mile radius of his home. He receives 25 or more assignments each year, mostly at small congregations that no longer can afford to support a full-time minister. He has made many friends at those churches, which request his return. Our mother, who died in 2020, always went with him to support him and, as he says, to offer an evaluation of how he ministered each day. He puts all of his honorariums for preaching into a special account, which he calls "God's Fund," which he uses to make donations and help people with special needs.*

Did you expect you would live into your 90s? To what do you attribute your longevity?

HARRY SR.: I think it was in God's plan for me to live this long and continue to be in fairly good health, although I have some health issues that go with getting old. Brother Ben died at the age of 92. My mother lived to be 102. I can't say why I'm enjoying a long life. I smoked for many years from my early teens and quit several times, once for ten years and then quit again in or around 1981.

HARRY JR.: How do you feel about outliving all of your friends?

HARRY SR.: It's not easy being the last survivor among many friends with whom Beverly and I were very close. As the years go by, the loneliness that goes with getting old and the consequences like living in a nice house by yourself in mounting years keep getting worse.

HARRY JR.: Do you regret the time you missed with your family?

HARRY SR.: A couple of times I wanted to get ahead, and that's why I worked so hard because I wanted to reach a point where I didn't have to worry about finances, didn't have to worry about paying bills and didn't have to worry about Beverly having what she should have had. And you kids didn't have everything. You know it. You had what we could afford, and that wasn't much.

I remember one Christmas in particular, we didn't have the money to get you guys the toys, and your mom and I went down, and we visited (our mother's older cousin) Margaret, and Margaret asked what I would like for Christmas. I said I don't want anything for Christmas, but I'd like to see the kids get something. And she went out and bought you that Cutty Sark (model), and she bought Barbara a Barbie Doll and something else. I didn't know about it.

HARRY JR.: Given how life started for you, how do you feel when you look back on your life? It's amazing how much you did. How proud are you of your accomplishments? What would you change?

HARRY SR.: Until I reached an older age, I never realized that the job I did meant so much to me. Now, I appreciate and firmly believe that the journey I was on somehow was part of God's plan for me to survive the hardships of poverty during my early life. Learning discipline and respect for others during my military service was the cornerstone of my career as a photographer and reporter. It was a special occupation that provided my family the comfort of a beautiful home, food on the table, and other essentials.

I was proud that my beautiful wife, Beverly, was a stay-at-home wife and mother whose dedication to God and her family of a loving husband and three children was respected by everyone who knew her wherever we resided. Through Beverly's expertise and training in home economics, our two sons and daughter are living examples of what results when there is parental training and a strong religious agenda surrounding the entire family.

What would I change if I had that opportunity? Absolutely nothing.

6

Getting to Know Him

For most of my life, I felt I didn't really know my father. Part of that was because of all of the time he was working and away from us. Perhaps part of it was that for many years he put up barriers to protect himself from people who would take advantage of him, judge him, and put him down. And that, no doubt, was a result of his childhood.

As children, my sister, brother, and I spent far more time with our mother and her parents than we did with our father and his family. Mom was there to treat our scraped knees, take us on walks and read bedtime stories. We had frequent sleepovers at the home of our maternal grandparents on South Eighth Street, where our mother had grown up, and we spent summer nights at the cottage they owned at Happy Hollow, just off the Trevorton Road.

Most Sundays, we went to church, then had dinner at noon at our grandparents' house. They positively influenced all of us, including our father, who became part of a close-knit family.

In contrast, I can't recall ever spending a night with my paternal grandmother. She wasn't absent from our lives, joining us for Christmas, birthdays, and other holidays, but there wasn't the connection that we knew with my mother's family.

That's easy to understand, given the family life my father had come from and the difficulties his mother faced most of her life. It wasn't a lack of love; it was a lack of time and attention.

As our father's job responsibilities lessened in recent years, we have gotten to know him better. We spend time talking about his childhood and other periods during his life. We ask questions, then listen as he reminisces. That's why these questions and answers are so important to us. We are thankful for the memories he is sharing now.

Better late than never.

HARRY JR.: Tell me about our mother's influence on you. What did you learn from her? Did you ever expect to reach 70 years of marriage together?

HARRY SR.: From the moment I met her on the cool Sunday afternoon of April 6, 1946, Beverly had a tremendous influence on my life. I couldn't believe that a young lady as beautiful as she was could have had any attraction for me, a gawky kid from across the tracks, still wet behind the ears, without any income to even buy her a flower for Easter or my junior-senior prom. I think I impressed her by just being myself, as poor as I was. I'm sure God must have had something to do with arranging our meeting and our eventual engagement and marriage, even though we were separated for over a year while I was serving an enlistment in the United States Army.

What is heartwarming about our early relationship is there were several young men in her life while we were separated by miles and miles, but we were still united by letters to each other every day. And finally, when I came home from overseas, I considered myself very lucky and again blessed by God to be the one she chose as her lifetime companion.

And during those 70 years and 11 months together, she had an enduring influence on everything in my life, from lending me money to buy my first camera when I began working at the *Citizen* to helping me make decisions about job changes and other matters involving finances and lifetime security.

We didn't have much money when we first got married, but Beverly had one thing that any young woman would like to have: She was beautiful and had the personality to go with it. I truly believe there wasn't anyone we met or were around who didn't have an admiring eye for her beauty and her feelings about life in general, even my oldest brother. She was very attractive and had charisma when we were with other people, but she never showed any personal feelings about it.

HARRY JR.: What was your greatest accomplishment in life?

HARRY SR.: Thinking about how I overcame poverty to learn a trade that today requires a special college education, as well as a desire by anyone to reach a goal in life, is what I would consider my greatest accomplishment. That I would be successful in journalism and photojournalism, despite several setbacks that almost caused me to lose everything in life I had gained, was something I never thought would happen. But only by the grace of God did I overcome some difficult times and continue to reach my goal.

I became religious, and to express my personal thanks to God, I studied theology by completing two years of training during my retirement to become an Authorized Lay Worship Leader, filling a need for qualified speakers to serve as supply lay leaders in congregations of the Upper Susquehanna Synod, Lutheran Church of America. That certainly would rank among my greatest accomplishments also.

And if there were a third choice, I would say accepting the challenge to research and write a book detailing the history and growth of Knoebel's Amusement Park for its 75th anniversary was another crowning achievement.

HARRY JR.: What was your biggest disappointment in life?

HARRY SR.: That I didn't answer God's call to become a lay leader long before I retired from the newspaper industry in 1992. The call was there long before I realized that God had a plan for me.

HARRY JR.: What bad habits have you had?

HARRY SR.: If you consider smoking even before I was a teenager, then that has to rank as one of the answers to your question. It was a way of life during World War II when all young men entering the military used smoking as a means of self-satisfaction and sometimes settling their nerves during tense situations. I finally quit for good several years before I retired from the newspaper job. And then there was a time when alcohol became a staple, and I found myself stopping for a beer on the way home after many night assignments. That caused a lot of problems, but eventually, I did a complete turnaround and thankfully overcame that problem.

HARRY JR.: What is one thing you would do differently in your life?

HARRY SR.: I don't think I complimented Beverly enough and didn't show her in a personal way how much I appreciated her as my wife, the mother of my children, and the many, many times she helped me with projects or other activities with my work as a photographer. Letting those you love know how much they are appreciated for what they do and what they really mean in your life is more than just saying thank you. It's telling them at every opportunity you get how important they are to you and showering them with gifts, even a single rose, as a token of your love. My heart aches because I know that in our long marriage, I missed the opportunity many times to take the time and put her on a pedestal for all the things she meant and all the things she did for me.

HARRY JR.: At what point in your life did you finally feel you had moved past poverty and were comfortable?

HARRY SR.: We experienced many hardships in our lives because medical bills, prescription drugs, and other expenses seemed to come faster than we could keep up with them in our early married life. Around the age of 45, I finally realized that I only had 20 years to build a nest egg for retirement. So I made a personal commitment. I would take all the extra money I made from freelance photography work, officiating high school football and basketball games, and any other extra income and deposit it in IRA and money market accounts. The plan materialized, and by the age of 65, I had enough saved for a reasonable monthly payout, augmenting our social security income.

I can truthfully say that since I retired from the newspaper, and despite the fact that a weekly or bi-weekly salary doesn't exist anymore, we have been living comfortably, paying all our utility and other bills, and enjoying enough income from investments to go out for an expensive dinner every once in a while.

HARRY JR.: Tell me about your first car. What was the favorite car you've owned?

HARRY SR.: My first car was a real dog. It was a gray 1940-plus Chevrolet sedan. I had problems with it from the day I bought it from Mertz's, a new car dealer who also had a used car lot in Tharptown, one block from my parents' home. I can't begin to tell you how much was wrong with that first car, but the big problem was that they couldn't find what was causing an oil leak. I had it for only a short time, after which Beverly's dad came to my rescue and directed me to a fellow he knew named Oscar Brown, who had a used-car lot along Trevorton Road.

He sold me a 1947 Chevrolet that was a really good buy. It served my purpose for a couple of years before Beverly and I decided we'd like to have a brand new 1954 Chevrolet that we bought from Fetteroff's on Spurzheim Street. That was a dream car, green and yellow with seats to match. It served us well until Beverly, while learning to drive, drove into an embankment on Badman's Hill in Irish Valley and crumpled the left-front fender. I was so upset, I got out of the car and kicked the fender.

So I ended up buying a 1957 Plymouth that was a real lemon. It developed transmission problems from the day I drove it out of the garage at a dealer's business in Tharptown. There were many other cars following that. Some were used cars; others were new ones. Since my retirement in 1992, we have purchase new cars every time we decided we needed a different car.

HARRY JR.: What was your favorite trip or vacation?

HARRY SR.: Israel was it. That was in 1996. Israel was very educational. You felt wherever you went, you were walking where Jesus walked. It was right after I had a turnaround. In 1989, I got that thing where I had that kidney stone, and they couldn't find it. I thought I was a goner. I had so much pain.

When I went to Israel, I felt that God blessed me. We took communion at the place where Jesus was crucified. Mom loved that trip.

HARRY JR.: You often talk about a special trip to Walt Disney World. Tell me about that.

HARRY SR.: Disney World was founded in 1972, and we went down when they opened it up for the first time. And then the 20th anniversary was 1992, the year I retired. They invited media people from all over the world, and they paid all their expenses. They flew us into Orlando. They picked us up on a bus. They took us to special cottages. It was a four-day affair, Friday, Saturday, Sunday, Monday. At nighttime, they opened the park up, and you had the run of the park. One night it was the park. Another night it was EPCOT. There were four different ones. They fed you, and they treated you like a king. They had celebrities Vanna White and Pat Sajak from the *Wheel of Fortune*. We were all in this big banquet with them. We were sitting within spitting distance of Pat Sajak and Vanna White. I took pictures of them.

That was tremendous. They had champagne at every intersection in Disney World. They had trays, not with cups, but with crystal glasses all filled with champagne. When you went back to the hotel room later that night, there was a gift there for you.

HARRY JR.: Share your favorites of the following:

HARRY SR.: **Bible verse:** John 3:16: "For God so loved the world that he gave his one and only Son, that whoever believes in him shall not perish but have eternal life." It is an assurance of an afterlife if we continue to believe in God's Son, Jesus the Christ.

Television show: Both Beverly and I have not liked some of the violence depicted on TV, so we were always happy to watch the game shows *Wheel of Fortune* and *Jeopardy*.

Book: Frankly, I can't remember what novel was the best that I read. But if you were to ask me what book I think is the best ever written, I would not hesitate in telling you *The Holy Bible*. When I was a senior in high school, I did a book report on *Mutiny on the Bounty* after my return from military service. Others had good plots, including *God's Little Acre*, *From Here to Eternity*, *Gone with the Wind*, and *War and Peace*, to name just a few.

Movie: No question about it, the best, in my opinion, was *Gone with the Wind*, a classic in cinema history from the standpoint of its production, as well as its depiction of the Civil War. The acting was super. I was only a little older than ten when I first saw it in the Victoria Theater. Another movie I remember as a young boy was *The Pride of the Yankees*, the story about Lou Gehrig and the honor bestowed on him during a tear-provoking ceremony at his last game in Yankee Stadium. His speech touched my heart, and I cried all the way home. If I had another choice, I would select *The Ten Commandments*, one of the best films by Cecil B. DeMille.

Song: The same week that Beverly and I met, we went on a Friday night date to see a movie at the Victoria Theater, and the title of that movie was *Sentimental Journey*, the same title of a song popular in 1946.

Food: I like prime rib now and then, but I also have a taste for chicken and waffles.

Dessert: Ice cream and strawberry shortcake.

Color: Blue because it matches my eyes. Purple is a close second.

Possession: The many awards I won and the commendations I received for my many years of work in the newspaper profession. They are on the back wall in my den, and every time I look at them, it's a trip back in time, reminding me of the hours I spent covering or photographing many events that were part of our community's history.

President: Jack Kennedy, with Ronald Reagan a close second.

Quote: From President Kennedy's inauguration speech, "Ask not what your country can do for you—ask what you can do for your country."[12]

Season of the year: I have many memories of the fall season because of the high school football games I officiated during 35 years. But I would join the majority who would pick the summer because of the warm temperatures and vacation trips.

HARRY JR.: What practical jokes have you played?

HARRY SR.: We had a chicken pen in the middle of our yard in Tharptown and a rooster that wasn't very friendly. In fact, you couldn't go in the pen without experiencing an attack from that rooster. Well, one day, I told Duke about the chicken and how friendly it was. He wanted to test the rooster, but once inside the pen, he quickly wanted to get out but, I had locked the gate. Fortunately, I unfastened the rope locking the gate, and he was able to escape without being flopped.

Another funny one was while I was on military duty in occupied Japan. Two of my army friends, Jim Brannigan and Benny Edwards, were with me in downtown Tokyo one afternoon when Brannigan decided to play a joke on the passersby. "Let's stand on the corner and just keep looking up at the sky," he said. We did. Within a couple of minutes, a crowd of about 15 or 20 civilians joined us and looked up at the sky too for a long time. We didn't see anything. It was funny because something as simple as looking up at the sky drew a large crowd to see what we saw—a couple of clouds.

HARRY JR.: After your children became adults and had children of their own, we shared a lot of fun times with you. What are some humorous family stories you remember?

HARRY SR.: My grandson Jason is a character who used to do anything for a laugh. One day during a family gathering, we were assembled in the den, and I decided to show some home movie clips about previous reunions on VHS tape. My youngest son, Terry, set up the VCR for playback, and it was going along fine for a few minutes, but then the picture started to get all kinds of lines and static in it, and it was hard to watch. I thought Terry had done something with the tape or the tape machine, but a short time later, I learned that Jason had the remote under his shirt and was causing all the problems just for a laugh and to see my reaction. His antics weren't centered on family gatherings alone. More than once, when his parents brought him with them to visit us, he made a habit of setting the alarm clocks in our three bedrooms to activate at all hours of the morning, starting at 2:00 a.m.

HARRY JR.: *One of our family's favorite memories involves one Christmas morning with my mother. She may have been the most giving and selfless person I've known. She was one of those who truly would rather give gifts than receive them.*

About 18 years ago, my father, who is not the best of shoppers, wanted to get mom something she really wanted. So he asked her, and eventually, she described a certain type of robe. Not wanting to take a chance, he enlisted my wife to help him with the purchase, but somewhere the description or the translation was mixed up.

Dad couldn't wait for her to open the box.

Her reaction: "That's not what I wanted."

It was so unexpected, so out of character, that it was the most fun we had had in years. Mom laughed too, surprised at what she had said. And we have remembered and laughed about it every Christmas since.

HARRY JR.: Have you enjoyed your children and grandchildren joking with you?

HARRY SR.: I would be disappointed even today if I didn't accept and enjoy all three of my children laughing at certain statements or words. I was always game for any event or talk that brought laughter to the kids and other members of their families.

HARRY JR.: Tell me about a few of the phrases you use frequently.

HARRY SR.: *"I'm too young to be a grandfather" (at the birth of your first grandchild, when you were 48):* It was my way of thinking that I was younger than I actually was.

"You're the best darn looking waitress" and *"I'm going to buy this place and give you a raise" (whenever we went out to a restaurant):* Going out to dinner was a luxury. I always tried to make the event fun by kidding with the waitresses.

"Get a haircut, you doggone hippie" (directed at me during my teenage years and my favorite of your phrases, especially considering later in life your hair was longer than mine): You're right. What else can I say?

"You're old enough to know better" (directed at me) and *"He's only little" (about our brother, who was ten years younger than me):* It was our way of keeping our youngest child from being shut out by his older siblings.

HARRY JR.: Do you believe you were tough on your children? Did your childhood affect how you were as a father? No one in the family disputes that you were less strict with our younger brother than with my sister and me. Do you believe you mellowed?

HARRY SR.: I don't think I was tough on my three children, but I did demand respect that I didn't have as a child or early adult, even extending in later years in some of the positions I held as an executive in my occupational career. I tried to teach them to be appreciative of the things they had: a good, caring, loving, and dedicated mother, a comfortable home, clothes to wear, food to eat, toys of every kind to play with, the opportunity for a good education and a weekly allowance, which they had to earn by doing small, household tasks.

They often upset me by their acts of mischief, which they thought were funny, but then I remembered that I did some of the same things when I was growing up, and because of that, I sometimes learned to laugh with them. Being honest was a very strict rule both Beverly and I demanded because I know that being poor and in need, I had many dishonest experiences myself as a child and that even affected me later in life. I didn't want my offspring to follow that pattern.

I credit their mother with always taking the time to instruct them about Christianity and the need to live an honest life. She set the example, and I sincerely believe all three children still to this day have followed her motherly teachings and advice and are following the example of Christianity they learned from their mother.

My role as a father and provider has caused me to mellow over the years, and although there were times I strayed, I realize that the only way to live a good life is to be kind and generous, especially to those in need, pray for the forgiveness of all wrongdoings and follow Jesus's command to love others as He has loved us.

HARRY JR.: Anything else you want to share about your children?

HARRY SR.: There has been a close relationship in our family from the birth of our firstborn, Harry J., in 1952, the arrival of our daughter, Barbara Christine, in 1954, and our welcoming another son, Terry Leroy, in 1962. Although the two oldest, Harry Jr. and Barbara, have a perpetual kidding about which is the "favorite" in the eyes of their parents, all three have been treated and loved equally and received all benefits we were able to afford. Terry's arrival eight years after Barbara's birth and ten years after Harry's was a joy. Beverly and I admittedly were a little overprotective of Terry, and when the older kids complained about him getting preferential treatment, we would counter the expression, "Well, he's only little."

It turned out to be a standard parental expression even after all three grew up and went out in the world on their own. After graduating from Southern Columbia Area High School, Catawissa, Pennsylvania, all had the opportunity to attend college. Terry declined and opted to enter the United States Navy for a one-term enlistment. Harry earned a degree in English at Bloomsburg State College, and Barbara completed four years of study at Mansfield University and became a registered dietician. Harry and Terry followed in my footsteps by working in communications, Harry completing a lengthy career as editor of the *Reading Eagle* newspaper, and Terry still involved as manager of radio stations in the Scranton, Pennsylvania, area. They all have families of their own, having children and grandchildren.

There are 19 great-grandchildren as descendants. I know that both Beverly, if she were still here, and I have always been proud of our three children and the ten grandchildren and great-grandchildren. God has blessed us with a beautiful family. Amen.

HARRY JR.: Despite how important your work always was to you, since mom died in 2020, it's become even more obvious to us how much she meant to you. If you could have one more conversation with her, what would you say?

HARRY SR.: I would tell her that I was sorry that I never told her while she lived how much I appreciated her for what she did for me. That's what I would tell her. I was loving, but I should have been more appreciative of her presence in everything I did, from helping me at weddings to standing behind me when I had problems, making sure I went to church and worshiped God, making sure I was the person she thought she married. I would praise her to no end for what she was and what she meant, not only to me but to you guys, the three kids. She meant a lot.

There were times when I couldn't have done anything without her help. If I had a project, she was there helping me. If I took on any extra work, she was there helping me. When I was training to be an authorized lay worship leader, she would look at my answers and tell me if I was right or wrong. When I went out speaking at churches, she accompanied me every time, and she sat there and would signal me if I needed to speak louder or slow it down. She wasn't educated in teaching, but she was my teacher, not only my wife.

She was perfect. She was the perfect person that I married, but I never told her that. I never sat down and said: "Honey, I want to say thank you. I want to say more than thank you." It's more than saying thank you—it's telling people how much you appreciate them.

Afterword

The poverty our father knew as a child wasn't something I could fully appreciate when I was a boy, even though I remember clearly visiting his childhood home, where he had experienced so many hardships. We didn't have everything we wanted during my own childhood, but we had what we needed. Part of what we had was because of the help we got from our mother's parents. The biggest reason was the hard work of our father to support and protect his family. I now understand that our father did what he believed he had to do—for himself and us.

Poverty didn't hit home for me until I went on several church mission trips to eastern Kentucky in the 1990s, where I witnessed generational poverty in that Appalachian Mountain region. I saw hopelessness in people who had no means to escape their circumstances. I could see and realize how far my father came in his life. Now, through this book, I have a better understanding of that life.

His journey has been remarkable and inspiring, especially since I've taken the time to learn about him. He is the reason I began my career in the newspaper business, overcame some minor challenges compared to what my father experienced, and eventually became the editor of the *Reading Eagle*.

He taught me dedication and commitment. Through him, I learned the importance of accuracy and trust. He instilled in me a work ethic to go beyond what was required and do a job the right way. And he showed me that no matter how difficult that task or assignment, I should never quit. Because he never did.

Several times while working on this book, my father felt overwhelmed and said he needed a break. One time, after a few days, I lovingly

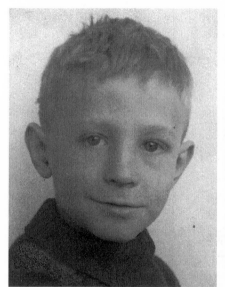

Harry Joseph Deitz, separated by almost 90 years.

reminded him that he was the one who taught me to stay focused on a job or project until it was finished.

I thank him for all of those things and for the special time we have spent working on this project together.

Given the choice to look back at the steps he took to escape poverty and build a stellar career or have memories of spending more time together and knowing him better, I wouldn't hesitate to choose the latter. Life doesn't work that way. We have to be thankful for what we have now.

In the end, the separate parts of our journey aren't nearly as important as the journey itself. Since our mother died, we have come to know and understand our father. These days, we spend more time with him than when we were children, even though we live more than an hour apart. We talk on the phone almost daily. He is genuinely happy to see and hear from us. Now he tells us he loves us. Frequently.

It's obvious he is proud of his children, and not just because he has mellowed. He has had a lifetime of learning the importance of family. Sometimes, he talks about regrets, despite the obstacles he overcame and the progress he made during his life.

"I should have appreciated her years ago," he says about our mother. "I look back and wish I had told her more how much I appreciated her.

But I got sidetracked. I should have spent more time at home with you guys, but instead, I was always out working, working, working."

I tell him we can't change all of that and that we need to focus on the present and on the positive things we've shared in life. The greatest example he gave to us was his love and devotion for our mother. They were married for 70 before she died in 2020 at age 89. She always was there for him. He always provided for her and us.

Since her death, he has visited her grave along the Trevorton Road almost every day. The cemetery is located less than 4/10 of a mile through the woods from where he grew up, or about a two-mile drive on the road from his house, about the same distance between his childhood home in Tharptown and our mother's on South Eighth Street in Shamokin. He says he feels her presence at her grave, especially when a breeze blows as he talks to her.

He continues to send cards and gift cards or cash at Christmas and for the birthdays of his three children, ten grandchildren, their spouses, and 19 great-grandchildren. He cooks his meals and tends to the flower gardens that used to be one of our mother's passions.

Now we see the depth of his love for her in the loneliness he feels since she is gone. The work and the chores he still does can't begin to fill the void in his life. He cries at times. He wants to be with her again. Someday, he will.

For now, he still has pictures that need to be taken, sermons that need to be preached, and children and grandchildren who need to know more about his long and successful journey out of poverty and the love story he shared with our mother.

It's a story and a journey that isn't finished.

A family portrait from the mid-1960s. From left, Harry, Barbara, Terry, Beverly and Harry Jr.

in 1999, the Deitz family celebrated Harry and Beverly's 50th anniversary during a weekend at the cabins at Ricketts Glen State Park.

Harry and Beverly Deitz, front, with their grown children, from left,, Barbara, Harry Jr. and Terry, during a 60th anniversary trip to Cape May, N.J, in 2009.

At a family wedding in 2011 in Seattle, from left, Barbara, Harry Jr., Harry, Terry and Beverly.

As a photographer, our father always paid attention to details, lining up groups so everyone's face was visible, including when we took family pictures.

The bond our parents shared and the life they enjoyed together became more obvious to us during their retirement years. They not only loved each other, but they also had fun together, as evidenced from their 60th anniversary weekend at Cape May in 2009. We all joined our father in laughing as our mother held up an oversized wine bottle, because she wasn't a drinker and seldom wanted to be the center of attention. Her greatest joy was taking care of her husband and children.

'I' before 'E' except in Deitz

By Harry Deitz
Regional Editor

SHAMOKIN — How would you like to wake up some morning and learn that you're not the person you think you are?

It sounds frightening, doesn't it?

I'm not talking about being an orphan or a ward of the court or anything else along those lines.

Somehow, I just knew it was going to happen long before I even thought about the possibility of retirement. But fortunately, there is still time to make whatever corrections are needed.

Harry J. Deitz

Let me explain in detail.

In English grammar there is the rule that the "I" comes before "E" except after "C." And therein lies the problem.

My concern started when I was awaiting discharge from the U.S. Army following World War II. Seated in the separation center at Camp Stoneman, Calif., I anxiously awaited the discharge papers, so I could sign on the dotted line and head for home after 15 months overseas.

When I scribbled my name, with the "E" before the "I" as I had done all my life, little did I realize the clerk-typist had written it with the "I" before the "E."

Well, two weeks later the whole mess was straightened out and I finally was discharged and was able to collect back pay and mustering out pay and everything else that was due me.

Now, some 40 years later, I already have started looking down the pike to what documents are needed for Social Security.

A baptism certificate will do. So, I made a quick call to the church where I was baptized. No problem getting the certificate. But, sure enough that "I" before the "E" cropped up again simply because the minister who baptized me and who, by coincidence had the same last name as mine, spelled his name that way.

Now, there might be a problem. After paying Social Security all these years with the "E" before the "I" my concern began to mount.

With that concern, I began to wonder how my name is really spelled. The answer could rest with the Bureau of Vital Statistics. So, off went an application to New Castle explaining the situation.

Three weeks later, the self-addressed, stamped envelope came back with two colorful birth certificates inside.

To my relief, the "E" certainly was before the "I." That meant the last name was correct the way I had spelled it all these years. There was no problem with the first name either.

But, how in the world the name "Albert" appeared in the middle name line instead of my baptized name of "Joseph" is beyond me and certainly is confusing to my 89-year-old mother who still lives in Tharptown.

One explanation is the old family doctor who filed information on the birth apparently was confused or just couldn't spell a simple name like "Joseph."

And the only other explanation is that somewhere else in Northumberland County, someone with the same first and last name as mine but with a different middle name was born on the same date. Sounds reasonable, but very unlikely.

I was informed in an accompanying letter from the Bureau of Vital Statistics that correction on the original record can be made. I'm in the process of doing that right now.

At any rate, my experience serves as a reminder to people in need of important documents for specific reasons. Don't wait until the last minute to get them. Do it now.

Scrapbook clipping from *The News-Item* of a column our father wrote in 1985 about the spelling problems with his last name. The spelling of Deitz has been a continual issue for all of us in his family.

Acknowledgments

Barbara Yates for family genealogical information, fact-checking, proofing, and overall support.

Shamokin Public Library for the use of *Shamokin News-Dispatch* microfilm.

Michele Ebert for information on the history of the Deitz family.

Mike Brown, an author from Georgia and a longtime friend, for his advice and direction in publishing this book.

Larry Deklinski, who owns the Thomas Studio pictures of Shamokin and the negatives from the former *Shamokin Citizen* newspaper, for allowing us to print several photos from the early years of our father's career.

The News-Item, Shamokin, for permission to use images of newspaper clippings.

Michael Gibbons for review and advice.

Edward Condra, publisher of the *Reading Eagle*, for permission to publish the column I wrote for Father's Day in 2012.

Notes/Photo Credits

NOTES

1. The Anthracite coal fields were located in Sullivan, Lackawanna, Luzerne, Carbon, Schuylkill, Dauphin, Northumberland and Columbia counties in the northeastern part of Pennsylvania, according to a 1916 report by the Department of the Interior, Bureau of Mines. Upper middle and lower. (From the Department of the Interior, Bureau of Mines report, "Coal-mine fatalities in the United States 1870-1914." Page 281)

"As of 2015 the Anthracite Region produced total of 4,614,391 tons of coal, predominately from surface coal mines." (From Pennsylvania Department of Environmental Protection.)

2. "Special tribute to a father who escaped poverty" was first published in the *Reading Eagle,* June 17, 2012, as one of my "Editor's Notebook" columns. Special thanks to Edward Condra, publisher, and the *Reading Eagle* for allowing me to republish it.

3. "We in America today are nearer to the final triumph over poverty than ever before in the history of any land." Herbert Hoover, speech accepting the Republican nomination, Palo Alto, California, Aug 11. 1928. From historymatters.gmu.edu George Mason University.

4. The date of his first day of school is based on the assumption that school started on the day after Labor Day, which was September 3 in 1934.

5. The Coal Township High School on Juniper Street was built in 1927. After the Coal Township and Shamokin school districts merged in 1965, it was used as a junior high and elementary school. It was torn down in 2000.

6. A sheeny in the 1930s community where my father was raised was considered a junk and rag collector. Many people now consider it a

derogatory or negative term referring to Jewish people. Given his family's poor circumstances, my father would not have used it as a derogatory term then or now.

7. The Graflex Crown Graphic is a large format camera that uses 4x5 sheets of film. It is often referred to as a 4x5.

8. Portions of this interview were recorded by my brother, Terry, during a conversation he had with our father.

9. This interview was recorded by my brother, Terry, during a conversation he had with our father.

10. The *Shamokin Citizen* continued to be published until 1967. The Shroyers Dress Company was closed in 1984.

11. Paul Vathis of The Associated Press won the Pulitzer Prize in 1962 for a picture of President Kennedy and former President Eisenhower walking together at Camp David after the Bay of Pigs invasion.

12. From John F. Kennedy's inaugural address, January 20, 1961.

PHOTO CREDITS

Page 7: Image of clipping of "Miner badly hurt in fall down manway" from March 28, 1930 *Shamokin News-Dispatch*, used by permission of The News-Item.

Page 7: Image of clipping of "Condition of mine victim is favorable" from March 30, 1930 *Shamokin News-Dispatch*, used by permission of The News-Item.

Page 30: Image of clipping of "Boy is near death result of being run down by auto" from September 26, 1931 *Shamokin News-Dispatch*, used by permission of The News-Item.

Page 30: Image of clipping of "Boy who was hit by auto recovering" from September 28, 1931 *Shamokin News-Dispatch*, used by permission of *The News-Item*.

Page 62: Photo of the original *Shamokin Citizen* building used by permission of Larry Deklinski, who owns the rights of the Paul Thomas and *Shamokin Citizen* photos.

Page 63: Photo of the *Shamokin Citizen* building used by permission of Larry Deklinski, who owns the rights of the Paul Thomas and *Shamokin Citizen* photos.

Page 85: Photo of the *Shamokin News-Dispatch* building used by permission of Larry Deklinski, who owns the rights of the Paul Thomas and *Shamokin Citizen* photos.

Page 87: Image of clipping of "Artificial Heart Valves Keep Two Women Alive," used by permission of *The News-Item*.

Page 140: " 'I' before 'E' except in Deitz" column from 1985, used by permission of *The News-Item*.

All other photos are from the personal collections of Harry Deitz, Harry Deitz Jr., and other Deitz family members.

About the Authors

Harry J. Deitz and **Harry J. Deitz Jr.** spent a combined 88 years working in the newspaper business—116 years if Harry Sr.'s post-retirement freelance work is included. Both began their careers as photographers in Shamokin, Pennsylvania, 25 years apart, and then became reporters, sports editors, and editors. Each has written a previous book. Harry Sr. was commissioned to write the history of Knoebel's for the amusement park's 75th anniversary. The *Reading Eagle* produced a two-volume collection of Harry Jr.'s columns written and published during his ten years as editor-in-chief of the newspaper.

Made in the USA
Middletown, DE
07 January 2022

58132767R00094